NORTHSTAR

Focus on Listening and Speaking

Intermediate

SERIES EDITORS
Frances Boyd
Carol Numrich

AUTHORS
Helen S. Solórzano
Jennifer P. L. Schmidt

 LONGMAN

NorthStar: Focus on Listening and Speaking, Intermediate

Addison Wesley Longman, 10 Bank Street, White Plains, NY 10606

Senior acquisitions editor: Allen Ascher
Development editor: Debbie Sistino
Director of design and production: Rhea Banker
Production manager: Marie McNamara
Managing editor: Halley Gatenby
Production editor: Liza Pleva
Photo research: Diana Nott
Cover design: Rhea Banker
Cover illustration: Wassily Kandinsky's *Im Blau* © 1998 Artist Rights
Society (ARS), New York/ADAGP, Pans; Transparency from
Kunstammlung Nordrhein-Westfalen, Düsseldolf, owner of the
painting, photo taken by Walter Klein, Düsseldolf.
Text design: Delgado Design, Inc.
Text composition: Preface, Inc.
Senior manufacturing manager: Patrice Fraccio

Photo credits: p.1, baby with legs © 1997, Comstock, Inc.; p. 5,
   professor lecturing class, Ron Coppock, Gamma Liasion ,Inc.;
   p. 81, Stephen Frisch, Stock, Boston, Inc.; p. 161, Arnold J.
   Sax/Coverage
Art credits: pp. 19, 23, 33, 59, 85, (right) 141, Lloyd Birmingham;
   pp. (left) 141, 152, Hal Just; pp. 77, 119, 157, 181, Dusan Petricic;
   pp. 57, 117, Andrew Techiera
Text credit: pp. 227, 228 Material adapted with permission from
   Car Talk®, produced by Dewey, Cheetham, Howe, all rights
   reserved. Distributed by National Public Radio®.

Library of Congress Cataloging-in-Publication Data
Solorzano, Helen
   Northstar, Focus on Listening and Speaking Intermediate/Helen
Solorzano, Jennifer Schmidt
      p.   cm.
   ISBN 0-201-57178-1 (pbk.)
   1. English Language—Textbooks for foreign speakers. 2. Listening
comprehension—Problems, exercises etc. 3. Speaking—Problems,
exercises, etc.
   I. Jennifer Schmidt   Il. Title
   PE1128.S26 1998
   428.2'4–dc21   97-41537
                                                   CIP

1 2 3 4 5 6 7 8 9 10-RNT-02 01 00 99 98 97

Contents

INTRODUCTION

NorthStar is an innovative four-level, integrated skills series for learners of English as a Second or Foreign Language. The series is divided into two strands: listening/speaking and reading/writing. There are four books in each strand, taking students from the Basic to the Advanced level. The two books at each level explore different aspects of the same contemporary themes, which allows for reinforcement of both vocabulary and grammatical structures. Each strand and each book can also function independently as a skills course built on high-interest thematic content.

NorthStar is designed to work alongside Addison Wesley Longman's *Focus on Grammar* series, and students are referred directly to *Focus on Grammar* for further practice and detailed grammatical explanations.

NorthStar is written for students with academic as well as personal language goals, for those who want to learn English while exploring enjoyable, intellectually challenging themes.

NORTHSTAR'S PURPOSE

The *NorthStar* series grows out of our experience as teachers and curriculum designers, current research in second-language acquisition and pedagogy, as well as our beliefs about language teaching. It is based on five principles.

Principle One: In language learning, making meaning is all-important. The more profoundly students are stimulated intellectually and emotionally by what goes on in class, the more language they will use and retain. One way that classroom teachers can engage students in making meaning is by organizing language study thematically.

We have tried to identify themes that are up-to-date, sophisticated, and varied in tone—some lighter, some more serious—on ideas and issues of wide concern. The forty themes in *NorthStar* provide stimulating topics for the readings and the listening selections, including why people like dangerous sports, the effect of food on mood, an Olympic swimmer's fight against AIDS, experimental punishments for juvenile offenders, people's relationships with their cars, philanthropy, emotional intelligence, privacy in the workplace, and the influence of arts education on brain development.

Each corresponding unit of the integrated skills books explores two distinct topics related to a single theme as the chart below illustrates.

Theme	Listening/Speaking Topic	Reading/Writing Topic
Insects	Offbeat professor fails at breeding pests, then reflects on experience	Extract adapted from Kafka's "The Metamorphosis"
Personality	Shyness, a personal and cultural view	Definition of, criteria for, success

Principle Two: Second-language learners, particularly adults, need and want to learn both the form and content of the language. To accomplish this, it is useful to integrate language skills with the study of grammar, vocabulary, and American culture.

In *NorthStar*, we have integrated the skills in two strands: listening/speaking and reading/writing. Further, each thematic unit integrates the study of a grammatical point with related vocabulary and cultural information. When skills are integrated, language use inside of the classroom more closely mimics language use outside of the classroom. This motivates students. At the same time, the focus can shift back and forth from what is said to how it is said to the relationship between the two. Students are apt to use more of their senses, more of themselves. What goes on in the classroom can also appeal to a greater variety of learning styles. Gradually, the integrated-skills approach narrows the gap between the ideas and feelings students want to express in speaking and writing and their present level of English proficiency.

The link between the listening/speaking and reading/writing strands is close enough to allow students to explore the themes and review grammar and reinforce vocabulary, yet it is distinct enough to sustain their interest. Also, language levels and grammar points in *NorthStar* are keyed to Addison Wesley Longman's *Focus on Grammar* series.

Principle Three: Both teachers and students need to be active learners. Teachers must encourage students to go beyond whatever level they have reached.

With this principle in mind, we have tried to make the exercises creative, active, and varied. Several activities call for considered opinion and critical thinking. Also, the exercises offer students many opportunities for individual reflection, pair- and small-group learning, as well as out-of-class assignments for review and

research. An answer key is printed on perforated pages in the back of each book so the teacher or students can remove it. A teacher's manual, which accompanies each book, features ideas and tips for tailoring the material to individual groups of students, planning the lessons, managing the class, and assessing students' progress.

Principle Four: Feedback is essential for language learners and teachers. If students are to become better able to express themselves in English, they need a response to both what they are expressing and how they are expressing it.

NorthStar's exercises offer multiple opportunities for oral and written feedback from fellow students and from the teacher. A number of open-ended opinion and inference exercises invite students to share and discuss their answers. In Information Gap, Fieldwork, and Presentation activities, students must present and solicit information and opinions from their peers as well as members of their communities. Throughout these activities, teachers may offer feedback on the form and content of students' language, sometimes on the spot and sometimes via audio/video recordings or notes.

Principle Five: The quality of relationships among the students and between the students and teacher is important, particularly in a language class where students are asked to express themselves on issues and ideas.

The information and activities in *NorthStar* promote genuine interaction, acceptance of differences, and authentic communication. By building skills and exploring ideas, the exercises help students participate in discussions and write essays of an increasingly more complex and sophisticated nature.

DESIGN OF THE UNITS

For clarity and ease of use, the listening/speaking and reading/writing strands follow the same unit outline given below. Each unit contains from 5 to 8 hours of classroom material. Teachers can customize the units by assigning some exercises for homework and/or skipping others. Exercises in sections 1–4 are essential for comprehension of the topic, while teachers may want to select among the activities in sections 5–7.

1. Approaching the Topic

A warm-up, these activities introduce students to the general context for listening or reading and get them personally connected to the topic. Typically, students might react to a visual image, describe a personal experience, or give an opinion orally or in writing.

2. Preparing to Listen/Preparing to Read

In this section, students are introduced to information and language to help them comprehend the specific tape or text they will study. They might read and react to a paragraph framing the topic, prioritize factors, or take a general-knowledge quiz and share information. In the vocabulary section, students work with words and expressions selected to help them with comprehension.

3. Listening One/Reading One

This sequence of four exercises guides students to listen or read with understanding and enjoyment by practicing the skills of (a) prediction, (b) comprehension of main ideas, (c) comprehension of details, and (d) inference. In activities of increasing detail and complexity, students learn to grasp and interpret meaning. The sequence culminates in an inference exercise that gets students to listen and read between the lines.

4. Listening Two/Reading Two

Here students work with a tape or text that builds on ideas from the first listening/reading. This second tape or text contrasts with the first in viewpoint, genre, and/or tone. Activities ask students to explicitly relate the two pieces, consider consequences, distinguish and express points of view. In these exercises, students can attain a deeper understanding of the topic.

5. Reviewing Language

These exercises help students explore, review, and play with language from both of the selections. Using the thematic context, students focus on language: pronunciation, word forms, prefixes and suffixes, word domains, idiomatic expressions, analogies. The listening/speaking strand stresses oral exercises, while the reading/writing strand focuses on written responses.

6. Skills for Expression

Here students practice related grammar points across the theme in both topics. The grammar is practiced orally in the listening/speaking strand, and in writing in the reading/writing strand. For additional practice, teachers can turn to Addison Wesley Longman's *Focus on Grammar*, to which *NorthStar* is keyed by level and grammar points. In the Style section, students practice functions (listening/speaking) or rhetorical styles (reading/writing) that prepare them to express ideas on a higher level. Within each unit, students are led from controlled to freer practice of productive skills.

7. On Your Own

These activities ask students to apply the content, language, grammar, and style they have practiced in the unit. The exercises elicit a higher level of speaking or writing than students were capable of at the start of the unit. Speaking topics include role plays, surveys, presentations, and experiments. Writing topics include paragraphs, letters, summaries, and academic essays.

In Fieldwork, the second part of On Your Own, students go outside of the classroom, using their knowledge and skills to gather data from personal interviews, library research, and telephone or Internet research. They report and reflect on the data in oral or written presentations to the class.

AN INVITATION

We think of a good textbook as a musical score or a movie script: It tells you the moves and roughly how quickly and in what sequence to make them. But until you and your students bring it to life, a book is silent and static, a mere possibility. We hope that *NorthStar* orients, guides, and interests you as teachers.

It is our hope that the *NorthStar* series stimulates your students' thinking, which in turn stimulates their language learning, and that they will have many opportunities to reflect on the viewpoints of journalists, commentators, researchers, other students, and people in the community. Further, we hope that *NorthStar* guides them to develop their own viewpoint on the many and varied themes encompassed by this series.

We welcome your comments and questions. Please send them to us at the publisher:

Frances Boyd and Carol Numrich, Editors
NorthStar
Addison Wesley Longman
10 Bank Street
White Plains, NY 10606-1951
or, by e-mail at:
awlelt@awl.com

ACKNOWLEDGMENTS

The authors would like to express their gratitude to the many people who contributed materials and ideas for this book. In particular, we thank Serena Coorey, Tom Scovel and Ray Solomonoff whose insightful interviews were the backbone for three of our units. Thanks also to the teachers and staff of the A.L.I. at San Francisco State University for helping us produce pilot listening tapes, and to the Students of the English Language Center at Northeastern University for their feedback on the manuscript.

Special recognition goes to our editors, Frances Boyd and Debbie Sistino, whose imaginative and sound advice helped to mold our manuscript into a text. And finally, thanks to David Schmidt, Roy Solorzano and Charlotte Mooers, for their support and encouragement throughout the process.

Helen S. Solórzano
Jennifer P. L. Schmidt

UNIT 1

ADVERTISING ON THE AIR

Can't keep up with the big boys?

1 APPROACHING THE TOPIC

A. PREDICTING

Discuss these questions with the class.

1. Look at the photograph. What product is this advertisement trying to sell?

2. This is only part of the advertisement. Look at page 2 for the other part. Now do you know what the ad is selling?

3. Look at the title of the unit. What type of advertising do you think this unit will be about?

1

B. SHARING INFORMATION

International Business Solutions can get you on the Internet in 24 hours.

e-mail

International Business Solutions

web page design

web site hosting

on-line marketing consulting

Helping small enterprises compete in the world of big business.

❶ *Look at both parts of the advertisement again. Discuss these questions in a small group.*

1. How does this advertisement catch your attention?

2. Why does this ad use a picture of a baby to sell its product?

3. Why is the ad divided into two parts?

4. If you were a businessman or businesswoman looking at this ad, would you want to buy the product? Why or why not?

❷ *What kinds of advertisements do you like? Look at the list of advertisement types. Check (✓) the three characteristics of ads that you like best.*

I like ads that have . . .

1. _____ funny situations.

2. _____ good songs.

3. _____ cartoons.

4. _____ nice-looking people.

5. _____ famous people.

6. _____ unreal (fantasy) situations.

7. _____ demonstrations showing how a product works.

8. _____ [other] _____.

Share your opinion with the class and listen to other students' opinions. What is the most popular type of ad in your class?

PREPARING TO LISTEN

A. BACKGROUND

Advertising has become a part of our everyday lives. Everywhere we go we see, hear, or read advertisements. Advertising companies do many things to encourage us to buy. For example, they write ads that include songs, funny situations, and famous people to make their ads memorable. Research has shown that these and other methods do indeed change people's preferences for certain products. As a result, companies continue to spend a lot of money on advertising.

❶ *Advertisements appear in many different places. How many different places can you think of? Work with a partner to fill in the list below.*

Places You Can Find Ads

Billboards (large outdoor ads)

Internet

_____

_____

_____

_____

_____

_____

❷ *The radio is a popular place to advertise products. Discuss these questions with a partner and report to the class.*

1. When do you listen to the radio?

2. Why would a company choose radio advertising instead of TV or magazine advertising?

B. VOCABULARY FOR COMPREHENSION

Read the sentences. Find the synonym or phrase in the list below that is closest in meaning to each underlined word. Write the letter in the blank.

a. have an effect on (something)

b. ways of doing things

c. ways to make us laugh

d. feelings

e. do one thing very well

f. the way we feel about ourselves

g. pay attention to

h. match

i. desire to save money

j. things that have power to make someone interested

_____ **1.** Advertisers use our <u>emotions</u> to encourage us to buy products. They make us feel happy or sad, for example.

_____ **2.** After seeing ads for milk, more teenagers in Australia started drinking milk. This shows how advertisements can really <u>influence</u> what we buy.

_____ **3.** Advertisers control our feelings by using emotional <u>appeals</u> that attract our attention.

_____ **4.** We all like to hear funny stories, so advertisers often use <u>humor</u> in their ads.

_____ **5.** It wouldn't be good to make a funny ad about a serious product. The two wouldn't <u>fit</u>.

_____ **6.** In the world of advertising, some advertising companies <u>specialize</u>. For example, some companies create ads only for radio while others create ads for TV.

_____ **7.** By emphasizing cheap prices many advertisements use our <u>thriftiness</u> to get us to buy.

_____ **8.** The goal of the advertiser is to get us to <u>focus on</u> the product. If we don't think about the product when we watch the ad, then the ad is not a success.

_____ **9.** Sound effects, music, and songs are different <u>techniques</u> that advertisers use to make their ads interesting and easy to remember.

_____ **10.** Our <u>egos</u> make us want to look good in front of others.

3 | LISTENING ONE: Advertising on the Air

A. INTRODUCING THE TOPIC

You will be listening to a lecture on advertising.

1 *Listen to the first part of the lecture. What will the rest of the lecture be about?*

2 *During the lecture you will hear some advertisements. Listen to the excerpts from the ads. What product do you think each ad is selling?*

Ad 1 Product: _____

Ad 2 Product: _____

Ad 3 Product: _____

B. LISTENING FOR MAIN IDEAS

1 *Listen to the lecture. Put the emotional appeals in order in column 1. Write 1 for the first one, 2 for the second, and 3 for the third. One of the appeals doesn't appear in the lecture. Then draw a line to match the emotional appeals in column 1 to the name of each product in column 2. One of the products doesn't appear in the lecture.*

Emotional Appeals	**Products Advertised**
_____ Thriftiness	Doggie's Friend flea collar
_____ Humor	Nexus luxury cars
_____ Curiosity	Younger You hair color
_____ Ego	Benton's Furniture

2 *Circle the correct answer.*

1. The professor plays examples of radio ads _____ the lecture.

    a. at the beginning of   **b.** throughout   **c.** at the end of

2. The professor presents the information in _____ manner.

    a. an organized   **b.** a confusing   **c.** a formal

3. In this class there is _____ participation from the students.

    a. a lot of   **b.** some   **c.** no

C. LISTENING FOR DETAILS

Listen again. Circle the best answer to complete each sentence.

1. Last week the class talked about the _____ of radio advertising.

    a. effectiveness   **b.** history   **c.** cost

2. Advertisers create humorous ads in order to help us _____ certain products.

    a. remember   **b.** ignore   **c.** understand

3. The Doggie's Friend flea collar has a _____ that fleas don't like.

   a. noise   **b.** smell   **c.** color

4. Advertisers *don't* make humorous ads for _____ products.

   a. expensive   **b.** funny   **c.** serious

5. At Benton's Furniture there is a 50 percent discount on _____.

   a. coffee tables   **b.** card tables   **c.** dining tables

6. The Benton's Furniture advertisement uses a _____ technique to encourage us to hurry to the store.

   a. countdown   **b.** singing   **c.** musical

7. People buy luxury cars so that they can look _____.

   a. strong   **b.** rich   **c.** safe

8. Kathy _____ a grandmother.

   a. is   **b.** is not   **c.** is hoping to be

9. It takes _____ minutes to get results from "Younger You."

   a. ten   **b.** seven   **c.** five

10. Tomorrow the professor is going to talk about _____.

    a. other appeals   **b.** other kinds of advertising   **c.** the cost of advertising

D. LISTENING BETWEEN THE LINES

Before advertisers create ads, they have to decide who the audience for their ads will be; for example, some ads are written mostly for women, some mostly for men, and others for either men or women.

Listen again to the advertisements from the lecture. On the chart check (✓) the characteristics that describe the audience for each ad. (You may check more than one characteristic for each category. For example, if you think the first ad is for both males and females, you should check **a. Male** *and* **b. Female** *in the section labeled "Sex.") In the section labeled "Other," write any additional ideas you have.*

	AD 1	AD 2	AD 3
Sex			
a. Male	❑	❑	❑
b. Female	❑	❑	❑
Age (years)			
a. Birth–12	❑	❑	❑
b. 13–19	❑	❑	❑
c. 20–39	❑	❑	❑
d. 40–59	❑	❑	❑
e. 60 or older	❑	❑	❑
Income			
a. Poor	❑	❑	❑
b. Below average	❑	❑	❑
c. Average	❑	❑	❑
d. Above average	❑	❑	❑
e. Rich	❑	❑	❑
Other			

Discuss your opinions with the class. Give reasons for your answers.

4 LISTENING TWO: Other Appeals

A. EXPANDING THE TOPIC

There are many other emotional appeals besides the three discussed in the lecture. The column on the right lists four. Listen to the following three ads. Match each ad with an emotional appeal and write the letter in the blank. One of the appeals does not appear in the lecture.

Advertisement

_____ Ad 1

_____ Ad 2

_____ Ad 3

Emotional Appeal

a. Fear

b. Desire for convenience

c. Senses (sight, smell, sound, touch)

d. Hero worship (admiring famous people)

B. LINKING LISTENINGS ONE AND TWO

Discuss the questions in pairs or in a small group. Then share your ideas with the class.

1. Think of all the advertisements that you heard in Listening One and Listening Two. Which of the ads is the easiest for you to remember? Why is it memorable?

2. Sound effects are often used in radio advertising. Which of the ads from Listenings One and Two use sound effects? Make a list of the ads. Then decide which ad has the most effective sound effects. Explain your decision to the class.

3. Do you feel that it is OK for advertisers to use our emotions to get us to buy products? Why or why not?

5 REVIEWING LANGUAGE

A. EXPLORING LANGUAGE: Sentence Stress

In radio ads, the actors emphasize certain words to help us focus on new or important information. This same pattern occurs in all kinds of communication. When we speak, we tend to emphasize certain words to make our meaning clear.

Listen to the following excerpt from the listening. Notice how the speakers emphasize the underlined words.

LIZ: It's <u>amazing</u>! You really <u>do</u> look younger!

KATHY: <u>Thanks</u>! Now people don't believe I'm a <u>grandmother</u>.

LIZ: <u>I</u> should try it.

To emphasize a word in a sentence, use one or more of the following techniques:

◆ Say the word louder
◆ Say the word slower
◆ Say the word with a higher pitch (tone)

---

1 *You will hear the following conversations twice. The first time, underline the words that are emphasized. The second time, check your answers. Compare your answers with a partner.*

1. KATHY: Hello?

   Liz: Kathy! I took your advice.

   KATHY: What advice?

   Liz: I colored my hair.

   KATHY: With Younger You?

   Liz: Yes! It's great!

2. KATHY: Did you hear about the sale at Benton's?

   Liz: Yes, I'm going today. How about you?

   KATHY: I think I'll stop by tomorrow.

2 *Practice with a partner.*

Student A:

a. Look at Advertisement 1. Underline the words you will emphasize. Read the ad to your partner two times. Emphasize the words you have underlined by saying them louder, slower, and/or higher.

b. Listen as Student B reads Advertisement 2. Underline the words that your partner emphasizes.

Student B:

a. Listen as Student A reads Advertisement 1. Underline the words that your partner emphasizes.

b. Look at Advertisement 2. Underline the words you will emphasize. Read the ad to your partner two times. Emphasize the words you have underlined by saying them louder, slower, and/or higher.

When you are finished, compare your answers. Discuss any differences.

Advertisement 1	**Advertisement 2**

Now find another partner and repeat the exercise. This time switch ads. (Student A reads Advertisement 2. Student B reads Advertisement 1.)

B. WORKING WITH WORDS: Word Forms

❶ *Work in pairs. Each partner chooses five words and looks up the missing forms in a dictionary. Share your information so that both partners can complete the chart. An **X** means that there is no common word form.*

Noun	Verb	Adjective
1. advertisement/ advertising	_____	X
2. _____	X	emotional
3. _____	influence	_____
4. appeal	_____	_____
5. X	humor	_____
6. thriftiness/thrift	X	_____
7. _____	specialize	_____
8. ego	X	_____
9. _____	create	_____
10. product	_____	_____

❷ *Work with your partner. Complete this letter by writing the correct word forms in the blanks.*

Dear Doggie's Friend:

I'm writing to let you know how happy I am with your

_____ . I heard your _____
　　1. (product/produce)　　　　　　　　　2. (humor/humorous)

_____ for a flea collar and decided to buy one. It's great!
3. (advertisement/advertise)

I don't usually let _____ _____ me, but
　　　　　　　　　　4. (advertisements/advertise)　5. (influence/influential)

the way your company _____ the flea collar was so
6. (advertisement/advertised)

_____ and _____ that I decided to
7. (appeal/appealing)   8. (create/creative)

follow my _____ and get one. Since then my dog has
9. (emotions/emotional)

had no fleas, and I'm saving money because this _____
10. (specialize/special)

collar is cheaper than the shampoos I used to buy. That's a big

advantage for a _____ guy like me. By the way, if you
11. (thrift/thrifty)

ever need someone to talk about the collar on the radio, you might

think of hiring me. I know this might sound _____, but
12. (ego/egotistical)

I have a great speaking voice.

Sincerely,

Alan Harrison

3 *The following sentences have word-form errors. Work with a partner.
Student A reads the sentences aloud with the correct word form.
If Student A reads the sentence correctly, Student B says, "I agree."
If Student A is incorrect, Student B says, "I disagree. It should be,
_____." Switch roles after item 5. Check your answers with
another pair.*

Example

The company decided to <u>advertisement</u> on TV.

STUDENT A: The company decided to <u>advertising</u> on TV.

STUDENT B: I disagree. It should be, "The company decided to
<u>advertise</u> on TV."

1. He laughed at the <u>humor</u> ad.
2. She <u>product</u> the ad.
3. He bought a <u>specialize</u> flea collar.
4. The president of the company is an <u>influence</u> man.
5. I like <u>advertises</u> that have good music.
6. My <u>thrift</u> mother always buys things on sale.
7. My job is to write <u>creativity</u> ads.
8. He's a very <u>emotion</u> actor.
9. The baby in the ad is very <u>appeal</u>.
10. This shampoo ad appeals to people's <u>egotistic</u>.

6 SKILLS FOR EXPRESSION

A. GRAMMAR: Imperatives

Imperatives are often used to give orders or suggestions. Advertisers often use imperatives to get people's attention and to make their message simple and direct.

❶ *Read the following excerpt from the* Doggie's Friend *advertisement. Underline the imperative statements.*

"Don't delay. Get a Doggie's Friend flea collar. It's available in most pet stores."

FOCUS ON GRAMMAR

See Imperatives in *Focus on Grammar, Intermediate.*

Imperatives

a. To form an imperative: ◆ Omit the subject ◆ Use the base form of the verb	"Get a Doggie's Friend flea collar."
b. To form a negative imperative: ◆ Put **don't** before the verb	"**Don't** delay."

❷ *Work in two groups, A and B. Each group stands in a line so that Group A students are standing opposite Group B students.*

Group A:

a. Choose a problem from the list on the next page. Tell the student in Group B (standing opposite you) your problem. Student B will make a suggestion.

Example

GROUP A: My dog has fleas. What can I do?

b. After Student B has made a suggestion, move along the line and ask the next student in Group B the same question. Keep moving down the line until you have spoken to eight students from Group B.

c. Decide what advice you like best and report to the class.

d. Choose another problem from the list and repeat the activity.

e. Think of a problem that is not on the list and repeat the activity.

Group B:

Listen to the problems Group A students ask. Make suggestions using imperatives.

Example

GROUP A: My dog has fleas. What can I do?

GROUP B: Try a flea collar. Don't use chemicals!

Now switch roles so that Group B asks and Group A answers.

Problems

My dog has fleas.

My hair is turning gray.

My dining table has a broken leg.

I get home late every day and never have time to make dinner.

I'm tired of work. I need a vacation.

I have a new car, and I'm afraid someone is going to steal it.

B. STYLE: Giving Instructions

Customers often want to know how to use a product before they buy it. For this reason, many ads provide instructions on how to use the products they are selling. To make instructions clear you can use **signal words**. Signal words are words that are placed at the beginning of a sentence to tell the listener that there is another step coming up. Here are some signal words you can use to give instructions.

Signal Words			
First . . . To begin with . . .	Then . . . Next . . . After that . . .	And then . . . And next . . . And after that . . .	Finally . . . Last of all . . .

1 *Look at the ad for Clayton's Chicken Teriyaki. The ad has instructions for heating the frozen dinner. The instructions are out of order. Work with a partner. Put the sentences in order by writing the numbers in the blanks.*

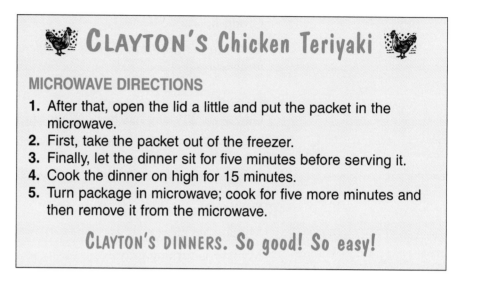

🐓 **CLAYTON'S Chicken Teriyaki** 🐓

MICROWAVE DIRECTIONS

1. After that, open the lid a little and put the packet in the microwave.
2. First, take the packet out of the freezer.
3. Finally, let the dinner sit for five minutes before serving it.
4. Cook the dinner on high for 15 minutes.
5. Turn package in microwave; cook for five more minutes and then remove it from the microwave.

CLAYTON'S DINNERS. So good! So easy!

Order of Steps

_____
_____
_____
_____
_____

2 *Work in pairs.*

a. Choose a product from the list below or think of another product.

b. Write an ad that includes instructions for how to use the product.

Products

shampoo	hair color
toothpaste	mouthwash
cake mix	pancake mix
tea bags	instant coffee
fax machine	photocopy machine

3 *Meet with another pair.*

   a. Read your instructions and ask the other pair of students to guess what product you're selling. If they are confused, ask them to explain why.

   b. Then listen to the other pair's instructions for how to use their product; guess the product.

4 *Work with your partner again.*

   a. Revise the parts of your instructions that were confusing to the other pair of students.

   b. Put your ad on a class bulletin board.

ON YOUR OWN

A. SPEAKING TOPIC: Creating Radio Ads

Work in a small group to create your own radio advertisement to perform for the class.

Preparation

   a. Decide what product you would like to sell and what it would be used for. Give the product a name.

   b. Decide what emotional appeal you will use (humor, thriftiness, hero worship, ego, fear, senses, or desire for convenience).

   c. Write the ad. Be creative! Use imperatives to make your message simple and direct (see Section 6A). Use language for giving instructions if your ad requires it (see Section 6B).

   d. Practice for the performance. Use sentence stress to emphasize important words (see Section 5A).

Performance

Perform your advertisement for the class. The other students should answer the following questions.

a. What product is this group selling?

b. What emotional appeal does this group use?

B. FIELDWORK

1. LOOKING AT MAGAZINE ADS

On Your Own

Find three magazine ads that illustrate some of the emotional appeals discussed in the unit (humor, thriftiness, ego, fear, hero worship, senses, or desire for convenience). Bring the ads to class.

In a Group

Show your ads to a small group of students. As a group, analyze each ad by discussing the following questions.

a. What emotional appeal(s) is the advertiser using?

b. Why is the advertiser using this appeal to sell this product?

With the Whole Class

Show your ads to the class and present the results of your discussion.

2. LOOKING AT TV ADS

Watch three different kinds of TV shows—for example, the news, a cartoon, and a drama. Make a list of the products that appear in the ads during these shows. Answer the following questions.

a. Were there differences in the kinds of products being sold during these shows? If so, what were the differences?

b. What influences advertisers to choose certain ads for certain shows?

Make a tape recording of your observations. Speak for three minutes. (When you make the tape, don't write out your comments ahead of time; just speak clearly and naturally.) Give the tape to your teacher for feedback.

TRAVELING THROUGH TIME ZONES

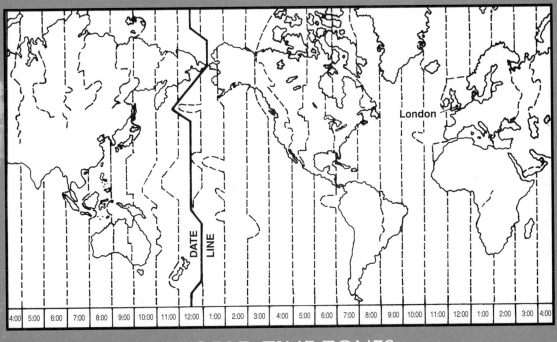

WORLD TIME ZONES

1 APPROACHING THE TOPIC

A. PREDICTING

Discuss these questions with the class.

1. Look at the map of the world's time zones. If it is 12:00 noon in London, what time is it in your city? (Hint: "West is less, East increase.") How can travelers use this map?

2. The title of this unit is "Traveling through Time Zones." What do you think this unit will be about?

19

B. SHARING INFORMATION

Discuss these questions in a small group.

1. Have you ever taken an interesting trip somewhere? Where did you go? How did you get there? What was the reason for your trip?

2. It is common for people to have problems while they are traveling. What is the worst problem you have ever had during a trip? What caused the problem? How did the problem affect your trip?

3. One problem people have while they travel is *jet lag.* Jet lag is a feeling that people get when they fly a long distance from one time zone to another. The change in time makes many people feel strange or sick for several days, until they get used to the new time. Have you ever had jet lag? What did it feel like? What did you do to feel better?

2 PREPARING TO LISTEN

A. BACKGROUND

Read the paragraph. Then follow the directions.

In today's international economy, many people have to travel a lot for their jobs. Business people, politicians, and airline pilots are a few examples of people who travel when they work. Although traveling is interesting, it can also be very tiring. People who travel long distances often suffer from jet lag. Jet lag can affect your work because it's hard to work when you feel tired or sick.

Work in a small group. Make a list of jobs that require a lot of traveling. Then think of the reasons why travel is necessary for each of the jobs. The list is started for you.

Profession	Reason(s) Why They Travel
Businessperson	To meet with customers in other places
Airline pilot	
Political leader	
Athlete	

Discuss other jobs that you can think of that require travel and give the reasons.

B. VOCABULARY FOR COMPREHENSION

Read the conversations. Circle the answer that best completes the definition of each underlined word.

1. A: Your <u>performance</u> in the last baseball game was excellent. You scored a lot of points and helped the team win the game.

   B: Thank you.

   <u>Performance</u> is _____.

   a. watching an activity   **b.** doing an activity

2. A: How can we <u>measure</u> the effects of jet lag on a businessperson?

   B: Well, we could count the number of physical problems a person has, like headaches or stomachaches. Or we could see how well the person is doing his or her job.

   To <u>measure</u> something means to _____ the amount of something.

   a. read about   **b.** find

3. A: Did you know that when people have jet lag, they have trouble thinking clearly?

   B: Really? How do you know that?

   A: I read a <u>study</u> written by doctors about the effects of jet lag.

   A <u>study</u> is a _____ about something.

   a. report of research   **b.** class

4. A: Do you know which baseball team won the World Series in 1960?

   B: No, but you can look in a book of <u>baseball records</u> and find out. There are records of who won all the past baseball games.

   <u>Baseball records</u> contain _____ about baseball.

   a. music   **b.** past information

5. A: My team played a <u>series</u> of games.

   B: How did you do?

   A: We won the first two games, but lost the last three.

   A <u>series</u> is a group of things that come _____.

   a. one after another   **b.** all at the same time

6. A: What are the <u>symptoms</u> of jet lag?

   B: Some people have trouble sleeping, and other people get headaches.

   A <u>symptom</u> is a _____.

   a. medicine used to cure illness

   b. physical sign of illness

7. A: I feel really homesick. I want to go back home.

   B: You haven't <u>adjusted to</u> this new place yet. When you are more accustomed to being here, you will feel happier.

   To <u>adjust to</u> something means to feel _____ after a change.

   a. comfortable

   b. uncomfortable

8. A: Do you believe that smoking causes cancer?

   B: Yes. Doctors have <u>proved</u> it. They showed people who smoke get cancer much more often than people who don't smoke.

   To <u>prove</u> something means to show that something is _____ true.

   a. definitely

   b. possibly

9. A: I want to play basketball, but I am <u>at a disadvantage</u>.

   B: What's that?

   A: I'm short, but everyone else on the basketball team is tall, so I can't play as well as they do.

   Being <u>at a disadvantage</u> makes it _____ to do something.

   a. less difficult

   b. more difficult

10. A: He's a real baseball <u>fan</u>!

    B: Yes, he really loves baseball. He goes to baseball games all the time or watches them on TV.

    A <u>fan</u> is a person who loves to _____ a sport.

    a. watch

    b. play

LISTENING ONE: News Report

A. INTRODUCING THE TOPIC

Listen to the first part of the news report and predict the best way to complete the following sentences.

1. The health report will focus on how jet lag _____.

   a. affects baseball players

   b. affects baseball fans

   c. can be prevented during baseball games

2. Researchers studied baseball and jet lag because _____.

   a. they are not interested in how jet lag affects businesspeople

   b. baseball teams want to know how to win more games

   c. it is difficult to measure how jet lag affects other types of travelers

3. The researchers found that jet lag _____.

   a. isn't a problem for baseball players

   b. affects some baseball teams more than others

   c. affects all baseball teams the same way

B. LISTENING FOR MAIN IDEAS

Listen to the news report. Read each statement and decide if it is true or false. Write T or F.

_____ 1. The study may help us understand how jet lag affects businesspeople.

_____ 2. Baseball teams from the West Coast win more games when they travel east.

_____ 3. The researchers studied the best-of-seven league championship series.

_____ 4. The symptoms of jet lag are stronger when a person travels west.

_____ 5. This study definitely proves that jet lag causes poor performance in baseball games.

_____ 6. Teams win more games when they have a "home team advantage."

C. LISTENING FOR DETAILS

Listen to the news report again. Choose the best answer to complete each statement.

1. Business travelers often feel _____ from all their traveling.

   a. tired and sick

   b. sad and lonely

   c. confused and frustrated

2. Researchers studied jet lag in baseball because _____.

   a. they are not interested in how jet lag affects businesspeople

   b. baseball teams want to know how to win more games

   c. it is difficult to measure how jet lag affects other types of travelers

3. Researchers analyzed the performance of baseball teams from
   _____.

   a. all over the United States

   b. the Eastern and Pacific time zones

   c. the Pacific time zone only

4. The San Francisco Giants and the Atlanta Braves played in the best-
   of-seven league championship series in _____.

   a. 1983

   b. 1993

   c. 1996

5. In the best-of-seven league championship series, the teams played
   _____ games in Atlanta.

   a. two

   b. three

   c. four

6. A shorter day is _____ to adjust to than a longer day.

   a. less difficult

   b. just as difficult

   c. more difficult

7. A symptom of jet lag *not* mentioned is _____.

   a. tiredness

   b. stomachaches

   c. headaches

8. This study does not prove anything because researchers only looked
   at _____.

   a. three years of records

   b. two baseball teams

   c. baseball players

9. _____ is *not* mentioned as part of the "home team advantage."

   a. Sleeping at home

   b. Hearing the fans cheering

   c. Traveling less

10. The health report tomorrow will talk about _____.

   a. how to prevent jet lag

   b. the effects of jet lag on business travelers

   c. jet lag during the Olympic Games

D. LISTENING BETWEEN THE LINES

Old or New Information?

When scientists make new discoveries, they need to consider past research or information that was previously known. When we hear news reports about new scientific discoveries, it is interesting to know what information is new and what was known before.

 *Listen to the following excerpts from the news report. Then read the summary statements below. Match each excerpt with a summary statement. Write the excerpt number in the blank. Then listen to the excerpts again. Look at page 27 and circle **New** if the information you hear is a new discovery, or **Old** if the information was already known. Write down some key words that helped you decide whether it was new or old information.*

Summary Statements

_____ **a.** Atlanta won the 1993 best-of-seven league championship series.

_____ **b.** It's easier for a team to win a game in its home city.

_____ **c.** Baseball teams from the West Coast are at a disadvantage when they travel east.

_____ **d.** Jet lag symptoms could cause poor performance in baseball games.

_____ **e.** The symptoms of jet lag are stronger when a person travels east.

Old or New Information?

Excerpt 1   Old   New

Key Words: _____

Excerpt 2   Old   New

Key Words: _____

Excerpt 3   Old   New

Key Words: _____

Excerpt 4   Old   New

Key Words: _____

Excerpt 5   Old   New

Key Words: _____

4 LISTENING TWO: Jet Lag in the Office

A. EXPANDING THE TOPIC

Listen to the conversation. Several office workers have just returned from a business trip. Match the name of the office worker with the symptom of jet lag listed below. Write the letter of the symptom in the blank. One symptom is not mentioned in the conversation.

Office Worker

1. Muna   _____

2. Jack   _____

3. Rosemary   _____

4. Marco   _____

5. Sarah   _____

Symptoms of Jet Lag

a. Trouble thinking clearly

b. Difficulty falling asleep

c. Problems doing physical activity

d. Headache

e. Tiredness

f. Stomach problems

B. LINKING LISTENINGS ONE AND TWO

Work in a small group. Discuss the following questions.

1. How is the information about baseball and jet lag useful for travelers who work in other professions?

2. The news report described how athletes who travel long distances by airplane have a disadvantage because of jet lag. What should athletes and sports teams do about this problem?

3. Would you like to have a job where you have to travel a lot? Why or why not? Discuss the advantages and disadvantages of traveling a lot for work.

5 REVIEWING LANGUAGE

A. EXPLORING LANGUAGE: Syllable Stress

Like other languages, English words have one or more syllables or beats. In English words, each syllable contains a vowel sound and usually a consonant sound.

Examples: *ball* (1 syllable)
base/ball (2 syllables)
per/for/mance (3 syllables)

In words with more than one syllable, one of the syllables is stressed. The stressed syllable sounds stronger (louder and longer) than the other syllables. Listen to these examples.

Examples: *báse/ball* (First syllable is stressed.)
ad/júst (Second syllable is stressed.)
per/fór/mance (Second syllable is stressed.)

1 *Listen to these words from the news report. Count the number of syllables and write the number next to each word. Put a slash (/) in between syllables. Then listen again and draw a dot (●) over the stressed syllable.*

_2_ a d/j u s t

____ a d v a n t a g e

____ d i f f i c u l t

____ d i s a d v a n t a g e

____ d o c t o r

____ e f f e c t

____ h e a d a c h e s

____ h o s p i t a l

____ m e a s u r e

____ p l a y e r

____ p r o b l e m

____ r e c o r d s

____ r e s e a r c h e r

____ s e r i e s

____ s h o r t e r

____ s y m p t o m

____ t i r e d n e s s

____ t r o u b l e

2 *Listen to the words again and repeat them with the correct stress.*

3 *Choose five of the words from Exercise 1. Write definitions of the words. Then read your definitions to a partner. When your partner answers, check his or her pronunciation.*

Example

STUDENT A: "Something that needs a solution."

STUDENT B: "A problem."

B. WORKING WITH WORDS: Draw a Word

Work in groups. First, write each word from the list below on a separate piece of paper. Fold the papers and put them together in a box. Then, one member of the group chooses a piece of paper. Without showing the other students the word, he or she draws pictures to explain the word, and the other students try to guess it. The student drawing the word cannot talk and cannot write numbers, letters, or anything in his or her native language. The group that guesses the most words wins.

doctor	series	tired	headache	researcher
trouble	travel	feel	hospital	short
symptoms	political leader	baseball player	measure	series
airline pilot	time zone	difficult	problem	

SKILLS FOR EXPRESSION

A. GRAMMAR: Modals and Verbs of Necessity

1 *Read the following paragraph about a professional volleyball player. Underline the words that show necessity. Then answer the questions below.*

Marta is a professional volleyball player. Her team has to travel from Peru to Spain to compete in the Olympic Games. There are a lot of things she must do before she leaves. She must not forget anything. Fortunately, some things were done by her coach, such as buying her airplane ticket, so she didn't have to do everything herself. Nevertheless, she has been very busy for the past few weeks. For example, last week she had to go to the embassy to get her visa. But because she did some things in advance, now she doesn't have to do everything at the last minute.

1. What is the difference between *have to* and *must*?

2. What is the difference between *doesn't have to* and *must not*?

FOCUS ON GRAMMAR

See Modals and Verbs of Necessity in *Focus on Grammar, Intermediate.*

Modals and Verbs of Necessity

a. To tell when something is necessary, use **have/has to**, and **must**.

- Marta **has to** go to Spain for the Olympic Games. She **must** do a lot of things before she leaves.

Have/has to is the most common way to express necessity.

Must is used most often in writing.

b. To tell when something is not necessary, or when there is a choice about doing something, use **don't/doesn't have to.**

- Marta **doesn't have to** buy her airplane ticket. (It's not necessary because her team can buy the ticket for her.)

- She **doesn't have to** do everything at the last minute. (She can choose to do things in advance.)

c. To tell when something is prohibited (when there is no choice about doing something) use **must not**.

Cannot is often used with the same meaning.

- Marta **must not** travel without her passport.

- She **cannot** travel without her passport.

d. *Must* can only be used for statements in the present and future tenses.

- She **must** practice everyday.

- She **must** get a visa tomorrow.

Use **have to** for all other tenses and for questions.

- **Does** she **have to** go to the embassy today?

- No, she **had to** go there last week.

2 *Work in pairs. Read the list below. Decide which things Marta* ***has to/must do****, **doesn't have to do***, and* ***must not do****. Check (✓) the appropriate column next to each item. When you are finished, check your list with the class.*

	HAS TO/ MUST	DOESN'T HAVE TO	MUST NOT
1. get a visa to enter Spain			
2. buy an airplane ticket			
3. pack her swimsuit			
4. bring her schedule of Olympic activities			
5. forget her passport			
6. carry her suitcases at the airport			
7. bring a gun on the airplane			
8. wear a seat belt when the airplane takes off			
9. talk to her teammate in the next seat on the airplane			
10. smoke a cigarette in the airplane's bathroom			
11. eat airplane food			
12. watch the movie on the airplane			
13. buy presents for her family			

3 *In pairs, discuss the reasons for your answers above.*

Example

STUDENT A: She must not forget her passport. She can't enter Spain without it.

STUDENT B: Yes. If she doesn't have it, she'll have to return home to Peru!

B. STYLE: Making Suggestions

In social situations and in the classroom, we often need to make suggestions. Here are some useful phrases for giving and responding to suggestions.

Giving Suggestions	Responding to Suggestions	
	Agree	**Disagree**
How about . . . ?	That's a good idea . . .	I don't think so . . .
Maybe (she) could . . . ?	OK . . .	I don't know . . .
What do you think about . . . ?		
Could (she) . . . ?		

Marta needs to pack for her trip to the Olympics. What should she take? Work in a small group. Take turns giving suggestions for things she needs to pack. Start by using vocabulary from the picture. Then, think of more items that aren't in the picture and continue your discussion. Make a list of the new items and present them to the class.

Example

STUDENT A: How about a toothbrush?

STUDENT B: That's a good idea. Maybe she should take some shampoo, too.

STUDENT C: I don't know. There'll be shampoo at the hotel. . . .

7 ON YOUR OWN

A. SPEAKING TOPIC: Discussing Jet Lag Prevention

Part A

Work in groups of three. Each student chooses to read a different section of the following article on "Preventing Jet Lag."

a. *Read only your section of the article. Do not read the other sections. Take notes on how to prevent jet lag using the chart on page 35. (Use **have/has to** and **must** in your notes [see Section 6A].) Take complete notes because you will be asked to share your information with the other students in your group.*

Preventing Jet Lag

Section 1: Before Your Flight
- If you fly east, go to bed earlier than usual for a few days. If you fly west, go to bed later than usual. This will help you sleep at the right time in the new time zone.
- Don't eat food with a lot of fat or sugar before or during the flight.
- Some people like to stop and rest for a day halfway through their trip, but it's not necessary.

Section 2: During Your Flight
- Drink a lot of water during the flight. You will need extra liquids because the air in the airplane is dry. Don't drink alcohol or drinks with caffeine because these take water out of your body.

- If you will arrive at night in the local time, stay awake during the flight and go to bed at your normal time in the new time zone.
- Set your watch to the new time about halfway through the flight. Start thinking in the new time.

Section 3: After Your Flight
b. Spend time outside when you arrive. Outdoor light will help you adjust to the new time.
- Go to sleep and wake up at the normal time for the new time zone.
- Don't do anything important the day after you arrive. It is difficult to think clearly when you have jet lag.

b. *Work with your group. Each member presents his or her summary. Use the chart on the next page to write notes for each section of the article.*

SUMMARY

Section 1: Before Your Flight

a. _____

b. _____

c. _____

Section 2: During Your Flight

a. _____

b. _____

c. _____

Section 3: After Your Flight

a. _____

b. _____

c. _____

Part B

a. *Work in two groups, A and B. Group A students are going on a trip to a country in another time zone and need suggestions about how to prevent jet lag. Group B students will give them suggestions. Start by walking around the classroom. Group A students ask five Group B students for suggestions.*

   1. Tell your partners *where* you are going and *why* you are going there.
   2. Ask for suggestions about how to prevent jet lag.
   3. Listen to the suggestions and ask questions.
   4. Thank your partner.

   Group B students give suggestions to five Group A students.

   1. Listen to your partner's request.
   2. Give suggestions. (Use information from Part A or think of your own suggestions. Remember to use the language for giving suggestions [see Section 6B].)
   3. Answer your partner's questions.

b. *Group A students report on . . .*

1. the most useful suggestion they received.
2. the most unusual suggestion they received.

c. *Switch roles and repeat the activity. (Group B students ask and Group A students answer.)*

B. FIELDWORK

1. INTERVIEW

Interview someone who has to travel between time zones for his or her job. Ask this person about jet lag and about what he or she does about it. Also ask for any travel advice that might be useful to other people. Then report to the class about what you learned. Use the chart below to help you write questions for the interview.

General Information

1. (Job) ?

2. (Reason for traveling) _____?

Jet Lag

1. (Symptoms) _____?

2. (Prevention) _____?

3. (Treatment) _____?

Other Travel Advice

_____

---

2. RESEARCH

*Look up **jet lag** in an encyclopedia at the library or on the Internet. Make a list of symptoms and ways to treat jet lag. Try to find information on new or unusual treatments (for example, melatonin, herbal remedies, light therapy). Compare the information you gathered with the information presented in this unit. Is it similar or different? Circle any new information you learn and present it to the class.*

TOO GOOD TO BE TRUE

Dear Antonio Mendez,

CONGRATULATIONS!
You are the lucky winner!

You have <u>already</u> won a
fabulous vacation to . . .

BALI!

To receive your prize . . .

1 APPROACHING THE TOPIC

A. PREDICTING

Look at the letter. Read the title of the unit. Discuss these questions with the class.

1. Many people get letters like this in the mail. What do you think you have to do to get the trip to Bali?
2. Do you think the letter is honest? Why or why not?
3. What does the title of this unit mean?

B. SHARING INFORMATION

The letter you read in Section 1A is an example of **fraud**. Fraud is a type of crime in which the criminal tries to cheat or trick you into giving money.

❶ *Work in a small group. Look at the list of different types of fraud. Discuss each kind of fraud and write a description of it in the blanks. The first one is done for you. If your group doesn't know about one of the items on the list, try to guess what it might be.*

1. credit card fraud   *when someone uses your credit card*
   number to buy things

2. sweepstakes fraud   _____

   _____

3. calling card fraud   _____

   _____

4. Internet fraud   _____

   _____

5. telemarketing fraud   _____

   _____

6. money-changing fraud   _____

   _____

7. mail-order fraud   _____

   _____

8. fortune-teller fraud   _____

   _____

9. marriage fraud   _____

   _____

10. immigration fraud   _____

   _____

❷ *Check the kinds of fraud in Exercise 1 that people in your group may have experienced. Then discuss other kinds of fraud that people in your group have experienced or heard about.*

③ *Choose one student from your group to be a reporter to present your discussion to the class. The reporter should answer the following questions.*

1. What kinds of fraud have people in the group experienced?

2. What are the four types of fraud that you added to the list? Describe them.

PREPARING TO LISTEN

A. BACKGROUND

Read the following paragraph and the two newspaper reports below about crime. Then discuss the questions on page 40 with the class.

Has anyone ever tried to cheat or swindle you (take something from you by telling you a lie)? If so, you have experienced fraud. There are many different types of fraud, such as credit card fraud and mail fraud. As technology increases, the kinds of fraud that exist also change. For example, we now have to be careful of computer and telephone fraud. In a crime of fraud, the criminal tries to get you to give your money willingly. People who are hurt by fraud give their money because they think they will get something in return.

Crime Report

Downtown Robbery

Linda Jones was robbed of fifty dollars yesterday in the downtown area. A man pointed a gun at her and demanded her money. Ms. Jones gave the thief her wallet, which contained fifty dollars and credit cards. The thief, a tall man with dark hair, ran away. Police are looking for the man.

Hospital Robbery

A woman came to Mr. Leo Chang's house asking for money to help a sick girl in the hospital. She said the money would help pay for the girl's hospital costs. Mr. Chang gave the woman fifty dollars. Later he found out that the woman had lied. She wasn't collecting money for the little girl, but was keeping the money for herself. "I was trying to help the little girl," Mr. Chang said, "but the woman stole my money." Police are now looking for the woman.

1. Both Linda Jones and Leo Chang were robbed. What is different between the two crimes? What is similar? Is one worse than the other? Why or why not?

2. How do you think Linda Jones felt after she was robbed? How did Leo Chang feel? Did they feel the same or different? Why?

B. VOCABULARY FOR COMPREHENSION

Read the following letter and the paragraph on page 41. Then match each boldfaced word with one of the definitions in the list on page 41. Write the number of the word in the blank. Compare your answers with those of a partner.

Dear Sir/Madam,

You have just won a **(1) luxury** vacation to BALI! You will stay in the most expensive room and eat the best food. We will treat you like a king!

To get your **(2) prize**—a free BALI vacation—please send a five hundred dollar **(3) deposit** right away.

With the deposit, we will send you more information about your vacation! (Your money will be returned if you decide not to go on the vacation.)

Sincerely,
Sunland Vacation Co.

You just received this letter in the mail. Ask yourself—do you (4) **trust** this letter? Do you believe the letter? Many people do, and they become (5) **victims** of a crime. Their money is stolen. Most people are very embarrassed to be victims of (6) **fraud** because their money isn't stolen by a criminal with a gun or knife. Fraud victims are often very (7) **gullible** people. They lose their money because they trust people too easily.

In a crime of fraud, the victim gives his or her money willingly, thinking that he or she will get something good in return. The (8) **con artists,** or criminals, don't tell the truth. They act friendly in order to gain people's confidence, or trust. Then they lie in order to get money. They (9) **put pressure on** people to make quick decisions and to send their money right away.

The best way to (10) **protect yourself** is to check carefully before you send money to a company you don't know. If you are worried about a letter like this, throw it away. Then you won't be a victim of fraud.

_____ **a.** easy to trick or swindle

_____ **b.** believe

_____ **c.** an award for winning a contest

_____ **d.** very expensive and comfortable

_____ **e.** strongly encourage

_____ **f.** stealing money by telling a lie

_____ **g.** keep yourself safe from danger

_____ **h.** people who steal money by telling a lie

_____ **i.** people who are hurt by a crime

_____ **j.** a payment that can be returned

3 LISTENING ONE: Too Good to Be True

A. INTRODUCING THE TOPIC

Listen to the beginning of the news report. Do the activities. Discuss your answers with the class.

1. Choose the best answer. This news report is about fraud . . .

    a. in a bank.   **b.** on the telephone.   **c.** through the mail.

2. Draw lines to match the names of the people in the news report with their description.

    Nadine Chow   Con artist

    Suzanne Markham   News reporter

    Frank Richland   Victim

3. What do you think is going to happen to Suzanne?

B. LISTENING FOR MAIN IDEAS

Now listen to the whole report. Read the statements below. Number the main ideas in the correct order. The first one has been done for you.

_____ Suzanne advises people not to send money over the phone.

_____ Frank asks Suzanne for a deposit.

_____ Suzanne agrees to send some money.

__1__ Frank tells Suzanne that she has won a prize.

_____ Suzanne says she didn't receive her prize.

_____ Frank says nice things about Suzanne to get her trust.

C. LISTENING FOR DETAILS

 Listen to the news report again. Circle the correct answer to complete the statements below.

1. REPORTER: In the United States, people lose about _____ billion dollars each year to telephone fraud.

   a. 40   **b.** 14

2. CON ARTIST: You have won a luxury car, $10,000 cash, or _____ cash.

   a. $15,000   **b.** $5,000

3. REPORTER: He is using one of the _____ frauds—telling the victim she has just won a big prize.

   a. oldest   **b.** most common

4. CON ARTIST: The first thing I'm going to need after you've won the prize is to put you on _____, to show you winning the prize.

   a. TV   **b.** the front of our magazine

5. CON ARTIST: To receive this prize, you must be _____ of our company.

   a. a customer   **b.** an employee

6. REPORTER: To get the money, the con artist has to get the victim's _____.

   a. trust   **b.** address

7. REPORTER: After he feels that the victim trusts him, the con artist puts pressure on the victim to make a _____ decision.

   a. careful   **b.** quick

8. REPORTER: What Frank Richland didn't know was that the
_____ were secretly recording the conversation.

a. television reporters **b.** police

9. VICTIM: But when I called the number, the phone had been
cut off. The company—Western Advertising Incorporated—was
_____.

a. closed   **b.** on vacation

10. VICTIM: Well, for one thing, the whole phone call was very
exciting, and Frank seemed so _____ at the time. So I never
really thought it might be fraud.

a. nice   **b.** gullible

D. LISTENING BETWEEN THE LINES

1 *There are a number of steps that the con artist goes through to get
Suzanne to send him money. The steps are listed in the right-hand
column, but they are out of order. Listen to the excerpts from the
news report. Put the steps in order from 1 to 5 by matching each step
with its corresponding excerpt. Write the numbers in the blanks.
Then listen to the whole news report again and check your answers.*

Steps in the Con Game

1. Excerpt 1   _____ Tell what the victim has to do to get
          the prize

2. Excerpt 2   _____ Tell the victim that he/she has won a prize

3. Excerpt 3   _____ Put pressure on the victim

          _____ Explain what will happen after the prize
4. Excerpt 4   is won

5. Excerpt 5   _____ Get the victim's trust

2 *Listen again to the excerpts from the news report, describing the steps in Frank's con game. At each step in the conversation, choose one or two adjectives from the list below to describe Suzanne's feelings. Write the adjective(s) in the column entitled "Suzanne's Feelings." Then write the reason for your choice. Discuss your answers in a small group.*

The following adjectives describe feelings.

| pleased | excited | happy | joyful | cheerful | confident |
| reassured | unsure | worried | frustrated | angry | scared |

STEPS IN FRANK'S CON GAME	SUZANNE'S FEELINGS	REASON FOR YOUR CHOICE
Tell about the prize		
Explain what will happen		
Tell about the deposit		
Get the victim's trust		
Put pressure on the victim		

4 LISTENING TWO: Other Victims

A. EXPANDING THE TOPIC

When we hear a story about telephone fraud, we often wonder how someone can trust a con artist. Listen to the interviews with some other people Frank called. Match the person's name with his or her reason for trusting Frank and write the letter in the blank. One of the reasons does not match any of the interviews.

Victim

_____ **1.** Joe Lau
Aged sixty-five

_____ **2.** Rosa Alvitas
Aged eighty-two

_____ **3.** Peter Alam
Aged forty-five

_____ **4.** Beth Goldberg
Aged thirty

Why the Victim Trusted Frank

a. The victim really needed money.

b. The victim was lonely and liked talking to Frank.

c. Frank put pressure on the victim to make a quick decision.

d. The victim trusted people easily.

e. The victim had never heard of telephone fraud.

B. LINKING LISTENINGS ONE AND TWO

Discuss these questions in a small group or as a whole class.

1. Think of the victims you heard about in Listenings One and Two. Who do you think is the most gullible? Why?

2. Could Frank Richland swindle you? How gullible are you?

3. People traveling to a different country often become victims of fraud. Why do you think this is so? What could international travelers do to protect themselves from being swindled by people like Frank Richland?

5 REVIEWING LANGUAGE

A. EXPLORING LANGUAGE: Reductions

In informal speech, some words are **reduced**. If a word is reduced it joins with the word next to it and the sounds change.

Example

Written English: Are you *going to* send the deposit?

Spoken English: Are you *gonna* send the deposit?

Written English	Spoken English *
I'm **going to** go to the post office.	I'm **gonna** go to the post office. (**Going to** is reduced because it is not the main verb in the sentence.)
I'm **going to** the post office.	~~I'm **gonna** the post office.~~ (**Going to** is **not** reduced because it is the main verb in the sentence.)
I **have to** get a prize. She **has to** get a prize.	I **hafta** get a prize. She **hasta** get a prize.
I **want to** win both prizes. He **wants to** win both prizes.	I **wanna** win both prizes. ~~He **wanna** win both prizes.~~ (The third person form [**he/she wants to**] cannot be reduced.)

* **Note:** The boldfaced words in this column are written according to how they sound, not how they are spelled.

Part 1

1 *Listen to the tape or your teacher say the following pronunciation chant. Snap your fingers to the rhythm. Pay attention to the pronunciation of the reductions.*

A: Do you **wanna** get a prize?
     Do you **wanna** get a prize?

B: Yes, I **wanna** get a prize.
     Yes, I **wanna** get a prize.

A: First you **hafta** send the money.
     First you **hafta** send the money.

B: I don't **wanna** send the money.
     I don't **wanna** send the money.

A: You **hafta** send it now.
     You **hafta** send it now.

B: I'm **gonna** call the cops.
     I'm **gonna** call the cops.

2 *Work in pairs. Student A is a con artist. Student B is a victim. Read the chant aloud three times. Start slowly and speed up each time. Remember to reduce the boldfaced words. Switch roles and repeat the chant three more times.*

3 *Work in two groups. Group A is the con artist. Group B is the victim. As a group, read the chant one time. Then switch roles and read it again.*

Part 2

1 *Read the following dialogue silently. Underline the verbs or phrases that can be reduced when the dialogue is spoken. Discuss your answers with the class.*

A: Hello, Ma'am? Congratulations! You're going to be rich! I have some exciting prizes for you.

B: Really? What do I have to do?

A: Well, first I have to ask you this. Which prize do you want to get: the luxury car or ten thousand dollars?

B: I want to get a new car, but I'd also like some money. Can I have both?

A: No, I'm sorry. You have to choose one of them.

B: Hold on. I'm going to ask my husband which one he wants! . . . OK, I'm back. He says he wants to get the money.

A: Great! Now, to get the prize, you have to send a small deposit of five hundred dollars.

B: OK. I'm going to the bank this afternoon, so I can get the money.

2 *Work with a partner. Student A starts the dialogue. Then switch roles and repeat. Use the correct reductions.*

B. WORKING WITH WORDS: Impossible Sentences

1 *Work in pairs. The following sentences don't make sense because the underlined words and phrases are incorrect. Read the sentences and discuss why the underlined words and phrases are incorrect. Then write corrections.*

Example

Incorrect: The <u>victim</u> stole five hundred dollars from Suzanne Markham.

Correct: The <u>con artist</u> stole five hundred dollars from Suzanne Markham.

  1. Incorrect: The con artist cheated Suzanne by telling her <u>the truth</u>.

   Correct: _____

   _____.

2. Incorrect: Suzanne knew that a luxury car cost <u>less</u> than ten thousand dollars.

Correct: _____

_____.

3. Incorrect: The con artist put pressure on Suzanne by telling her to make a <u>careful</u> decision.

Correct: _____

_____.

4. Incorrect: Suzanne <u>didn't trust</u> the con artist, so she sent him the money.

Correct: _____

_____.

5. Incorrect: Suzanne was gullible. She <u>didn't believe anything</u> the con artist said.

Correct: _____

_____.

6. Incorrect: Suzanne sent the money because she wanted to win a grand <u>deposit</u>.

Correct: _____

_____.

7. Incorrect: The <u>victim</u> arrested the con artist.

Correct: _____

_____.

8. Incorrect: Con artists are <u>honest</u> people.

Correct: _____

_____.

9. Incorrect: In a crime of fraud, the victim <u>knows</u> that he or she is being cheated.

Correct: _____

_____.

10. Incorrect: You can protect yourself from crime if you <u>aren't</u> careful.

Correct: _____

_____.

2 *Have you (or has someone you know) ever been a victim of fraud or trusted someone dishonest? In pairs, describe your experiences using the vocabulary from the unit.*

Tell your partner about a time when . . .

a. someone stole something from you (or someone you know).

b. someone put pressure on you to do something.

c. someone cheated you.

d. you were concerned about someone in trouble.

e. you trusted someone, but it was a mistake.

f. you protected yourself against a crime.

6 SKILLS FOR EXPRESSION

A. GRAMMAR: Comparatives and Equatives

1 *In the following conversation, two people are comparing fraud with other kinds of crime. Notice the comparatives (words that talk about more or less) and the equatives (words that talk about things that are equal). Then answer the questions below.*

A: A woman stole fifty dollars from me. I gave her the money because she said it would help a sick girl in the hospital.

B: That's a terrible crime. It's *worse than* being robbed by someone with a gun!

A: Well, it's *not as dangerous as* being robbed by someone with a gun.

B: Yes, but in the future you will be *less trusting than* before.

A: That's true. I guess fraud is just *as bad as* other types of crime.

1. Which of the phrases expresses the idea that two things are *equal*?

2. Which of the phrases expresses the idea of *more*?

3. Which of the phrases expresses the idea of *less*?

FOCUS ON GRAMMAR | **Equatives and Comparatives**

See Equatives and Comparatives in *Focus on Grammar, Intermediate.*

a. To express the idea of equal: ◆ Use *as + adjective + as*	Con artists are **as bad as** criminals with guns. (Con artists and criminals are equally bad.)
b. To express the idea of more: ◆ Use **adjective + -er + than** with one-syllable adjectives (Sometimes there are spelling changes when you add *-er.* If an adjective ends in *-y,* change the *-y* to *-i* and then add *-er.*) ◆ Use *more + adjective + than* with adjectives that have two or more syllables	Con artists are **smarter than** their victims. (Bank robbers are **scarier** than con artists.) Telephone fraud is **more common than** bank robbery.
c. To express the idea of less: ◆ Use *less + adjective + than* ◆ Use *not as + adjective + as*	Bank robbery is **less common than** telephone fraud. Con artists are **not as dangerous as** criminals with guns.
There are some irregular comparative forms.	**adjective** **comparative** bad → worse good → better

❷ *Work with a partner. Student A makes a statement comparing two kinds of criminals. Student B listens, agrees/disagrees, and tells why. Switch roles after item 5.*

Example

Bank robbers are _____ telephone con artists. (frightening)

STUDENT A: Bank robbers are <u>more frightening than</u> telephone con artists.

STUDENT B: I agree because bank robbers usually carry guns and telephone con artists don't.

   1. Bank robbers are _____ telephone con artists. (dangerous)

2. Shoplifters are _____ bank robbers. (frightening)

3. Car thieves are _____ telephone con artists. (hard to catch)

4. Bank robbers are _____ telephone con artists. (bad)

5. Car thieves are _____ shoplifters. (difficult to stop)

6. Telephone con artists are _____ shoplifters. (dishonest)

7. Bank robbers are _____ car thieves. (scary)

8. Shoplifters are _____ telephone con artists. (smart)

9. Car thieves are _____ bank robbers. (frightening)

10. Shoplifters are _____ bank robbers. (harmful)

B. STYLE: Expressing and Asking for Opinions

People usually have strong opinions about fraud. You can express your opinions and ask for your classmates' opinions by using the language below.

Expressing Your Opinion	Asking for Opinions
I think (that) . . .	What do you think, [name]?
I believe (that) . . .	Do you agree, [name]?
In my opinion, . . .	How about you, [name]?
	What's your opinion about this, [name]?

Work in groups of three to five students. Choose a discussion leader. The leader chooses one of the five statements below to lead a discussion on, states his or her opinion about the statement, and explains it. Then the leader asks each person in the group for an opinion. Each student in the group has a chance to lead a discussion.

Example

LEADER: I think that you should never give out your credit card number over the phone because. . . . What do you think, Soo-Mi?

SOO-MI: I disagree. In my opinion . . . .

LEADER: How about you, Maria?

MARIA: I agree with Soo Mi. I think that . . . .

Statements for Discussion

1. You should never give out your credit card number over the phone.

2. Victims of telephone fraud are not very intelligent.

3. Telephone fraud is a more serious crime than shoplifting.

4. Telephone con artists should go to jail for their crimes.

5. People should always report telephone fraud to the police.

ON YOUR OWN

A. SPEAKING TOPIC: Ranking Dishonest Activities

❶ *There are many kinds of dishonest activities. Telephone fraud is one of the more serious offenses (crimes). Evaluate the situations on page 55 and rate them from 1 to 10. Put 1 next to the situation that you think is the most serious offense, and 10 next to the one that you think is the least serious offense. Then, in a small group, compare your opinions and reasons. (Remember to use language for comparing and giving opinions [see Section 6].)*

_____ **a.** Lying about your work experience in order to get a job

_____ **b.** Pretending that you have something else to do so that you don't have to attend a boring office party

_____ **c.** Pretending to be poor so the government will give you money

_____ **d.** Lying about your health so you don't have to go into the army

_____ **e.** Taking money out of someone else's bank account

_____ **f.** Telling someone to send you money for a prize that doesn't exist

_____ **g.** Finding a wallet with money in it, but not returning it when the owner tells you it's lost

_____ **h.** Not saying anything if a store clerk gives you too much change by mistake

_____ **i.** Cheating on a test

_____ **j.** Selling something that you know will break soon

2 _Work in a small group. Look again at the list of dishonest situations._
How should people be punished for doing these things? Use the list
below to choose an appropriate punishment for each situation.
Write the letter for each situation in one of the columns. Present
your group's ideas to the class. Be prepared to give reasons for
your choices.

Go to jail	Lose your job/school position	Pay some money	No punishment	Other (Be prepared to explain)

B. FIELDWORK

1. WATCHING A MOVIE

There are a lot of movies about fraud, such as Paper Moon, The Sting, Wall Street, *and* The Firm. *With your class, watch a movie that deals with fraud. (You can go to a movie theater together or watch a video in class.) Meet in a small group and discuss the following questions. Be prepared to report to the whole class on one or more of the questions.*

a. What is this movie about? (Summarize it in one or two sentences.)

b. Who got cheated?

c. How did they get cheated?

d. Why did they get cheated? Could they have avoided getting swindled? If so, how?

e. Have you heard of a fraudulent situation similar to the one in the movie? If so, what happened?

f. Did you enjoy the movie? Why or why not?

2. RESEARCH

At the beginning of this unit, you discussed different kinds of fraud. Look back at the list of fraudulent activities in Section 1B. Choose one topic to research. Go to the library and look up your topic in an encyclopedia or on the Internet. Use these questions to help you with your research:

a. What is _____ ?

b. How many people in the United States and/or your country get cheated by this type of fraud every year?

c. How do criminals who are involved in _____ get you to give them your money?

d. How can you protect yourself from _____ ?

Meet in a small group with people who chose a different topic from you. Present your research to help warn your classmates about ways they can get swindled.

IF YOU CAN'T
BEAT 'EM, JOIN 'EM

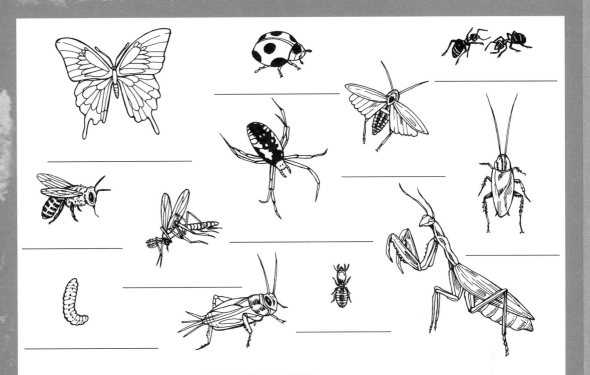

1 APPROACHING THE TOPIC

A. PREDICTING

1 There are twelve insects in the picture above. Write the name of each insect under its picture.

ant	cricket	ladybug	praying mantis
bee	cockroach	maggot	spider*
butterfly	firefly	mosquito	termite

2 Look at the title. What do you think it means? What do you think this unit will be about?

*Note: Spiders are not technically insects since insects have six legs and bodies that are divided into three parts. However, people often think of spiders as insects.

B. SHARING INFORMATION

① *Work in a small group. Look again at the insects on page 57 and divide them into categories. In the left-hand column, write the names of the insects that are harmful to people. In the right-hand column, write the names of the insects that are useful to people. Explain your answers to the class.*

HARMFUL INSECTS	USEFUL INSECTS

② *Repeat the exercise using different categories. In the left-hand column, write the names of the insects that are beautiful. In the right-hand column, write the names of the insects that are ugly. Explain your answers to the class.*

BEAUTIFUL INSECTS	UGLY INSECTS

PREPARING TO LISTEN

A. BACKGROUND

Read the paragraphs. Then follow the instructions.

Insects are an important part of life on earth. There are more than one million kinds of insects in the world—more than all other kinds of animals combined. Insects have many different living and eating habits. Some live in hot climates; others prefer cool temperatures. Some eat plants; others eat other insects or dead animals.

Many insects are useful to humans. For example, some farmers put ladybugs or praying mantises on their plants because these insects eat insects that destroy crops. However, insects inside a house are usually not useful. Termites, for instance, eat the wood in our houses, and ants get into our food. Most people want to get rid of, or kill, insects in their homes.

1 *There are many ways to get rid of insects inside a house. Match the picture with the name of the method. Write the answers in the blanks.*

Method

_____ **1.** fly swatter

_____ **2.** insect trap

_____ **3.** insecticide (poison)

_____ **4.** exterminator

_____ **5.** moving out of your house

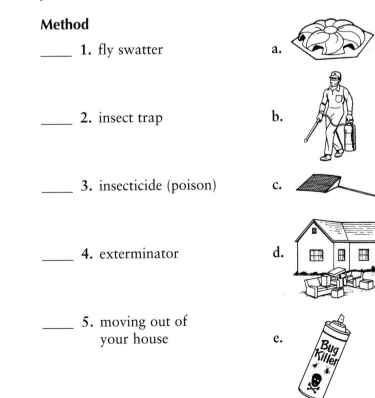

a.

b.

c.

d.

e.

2 *What is the best way to get rid of insects at home? Work in groups. Evaluate the methods of getting rid of insects in Exercise 1. Answer the questions about each method. The first one is started for you. What are other ways to get rid of insects? Add one other way.*

	METHOD 1	METHOD 2	METHOD 3	METHOD 4	METHOD 5	_____ (Add your own.)
Use: For which insects?	fireflies bees					
Effectiveness: Does it get rid of the insects?	some of them					
Safety: Is it safe for people?	yes					
Cost: Is it expensive or inexpensive?						
Effort: Is it easy?						

3 *Have you ever had a problem with insects? What type of insects? How did you get rid of them?*

B. VOCABULARY FOR COMPREHENSION

Match the underlined words with their definitions from the list.
Write the letter in the blank.

a. many

b. a test to answer a scientific question

c. groups of people (animals or insects) of the same age

d. produced an egg

e. continued to live; did not die

f. understand by thinking

g. not a success

h. helps animals produce babies

i. acting in a way you don't expect

j. taught

_____ 1. The farmer <u>breeds</u> cows. He sells some of the baby cows, and keeps others on his farm.

_____ 2. After the chicken <u>laid an egg</u>, the farmer collected it and ate the egg for breakfast.

_____ 3. My sister's dog ate some poison, got sick, and almost died. Luckily, he <u>survived</u>, and now he's healthy again.

_____ 4. She <u>trained</u> her dog to do many things. Her dog can sit, stand on two legs, and roll over.

_____ 5. The scientists did an <u>experiment</u> with vitamins. They tried to find out if vitamins will keep people healthy.

_____ 6. After the experiment was finished, the scientists looked at the results and tried to <u>figure out</u> the answers to their questions.

_____ 7. The experiment was a <u>failure</u>. The scientists didn't get the results they needed.

_____ 8. My friend lives with his grandmother, his parents, and his son. There are four <u>generations</u> living together in his house.

_____ 9. Whenever I visit my friend I bring <u>a whole bunch</u> of presents. I have to bring so many because there are so many people living in his house.

_____ 10. Sometimes her dog listens to her and sometimes he doesn't. He is <u>unpredictable</u>.

LISTENING ONE: "If You Can't Beat 'Em, Join 'Em!"

A. INTRODUCING THE TOPIC

Listen to Dr. Richard Solomon, an entomologist, talking about breeding and training.

1. What do you think Dr. Solomon is talking about?

2. What do you think an entomologist does?

B. LISTENING FOR MAIN IDEAS

Now listen to the whole interview. Read the statements below. Number the main ideas in the correct order. The first one has been done for you.

_____ The cockroaches in the experiment died.

_____ Dr. Solomon decided to breed the cockroaches.

_____ Dr. Solomon collected the cockroaches.

_____ Dr. Solomon tried to get rid of the cockroaches.

__1__ Dr. Solomon had cockroaches in his apartment.

_____ The cockroaches in the apartment did not die.

_____ Dr. Solomon fed the cockroaches.

C. LISTENING FOR DETAILS

Read the items. Listen to the interview again. Circle the best answer. Check your answers with a partner.

1. Dr. Solomon is _____.

a. a scientist who studies insects

b. an exterminator who kills insects

c. a reporter who writes about insects

2. The cockroach experiment took place when Dr. Solomon was a _____.

   a. scientist   **b.** college student   **c.** child

3. Dr. Solomon tried to get rid of the cockroaches in his apartment by putting out _____.

   a. poison   **b.** insect traps   **c.** water

4. Dr. Solomon decided to breed cockroaches because they are _____.

   a. smart   **b.** interesting   **c.** useful

5. Dr. Solomon wanted to train the cockroaches to _____.

   a. remember things   **b.** leave his apartment   **c.** carry things on their backs

6. Dr. Solomon kept cockroaches in a _____.

   a. bowl   **b.** box   **c.** jar

7. Dr. Solomon fed the cockroaches sugar, fruit, and _____.

   a. fish food   **b.** dog food   **c.** cat food

8. His experiment was unsuccessful because most of the cockroaches _____.

   a. died after one generation   **b.** jumped out of the jar   **c.** couldn't learn how to do things

9. From his experience, Dr. Solomon learned that _____.

   a. cockroaches aren't very smart   **b.** experiments with insects are easy   **c.** he was interested in studying insects

10. Dr. Solomon thinks that the best way to get rid of cockroaches is to _____.

    a. breed them   **b.** move   **c.** feed them

D. LISTENING BETWEEN THE LINES

 ❶ Read the statements. Then listen to excerpts from the interview. Do you think that Dr. Solomon would agree or disagree with the statements? Check the appropriate column.

DR. SOLOMON'S OPINION

	Agree	Disagree
Excerpt 1		
a. Today there are very good ways to get rid of insects.		
b. If something is impossible, stop trying to do it.		
Excerpt 2		
a. Cockroaches are smarter than most other insects.		
b. Cockroaches can be useful to humans in some way.		
Excerpt 3		
a. You don't learn anything when an experiment is a failure.		
b. Dr. Solomon always likes to know what will happen next in his experiments.		

❷ Compare your answers with those of your classmates. Did you choose the same answers? Explain why you chose your answers.

4 LISTENING TWO: Useful Insects

A. EXPANDING THE TOPIC

Dr. Solomon tried to solve his problem with cockroaches in an unusual and interesting way. Other scientists are looking at new ways of solving modern problems by using insects.

1 *Listen to the news report about using four insects to solve modern problems. Some of the information is true and some isn't. Draw lines to connect each insect to the solution and place described in the report.*

Solution	Insect	Place
Bring medicine to people	Maggots	In a hospital
Used in medical tests	Mosquitoes	In poor countries
Eat dead skin on an injury	Termites	Far away from doctors
Add protein to food	Fireflies	In a scientific laboratory

2 *Listen again to the news report. Some of the solutions described in the report are true, and some are false. In a small group, decide which solutions are true and which are false. Share your decision with the class and explain the reasons for your opinions.*

B. LINKING LISTENINGS ONE AND TWO

Discuss the answers to these questions with the class.

1. What do you think of Dr. Solomon? Does his personality seem a little unusual to you? What do you think of his solution to the cockroach problem?

2. The title of this unit is "If you can't beat 'em, join 'em." What do you think this means? How does this statement relate to Listening One? How does it relate to Listening Two? Do you agree with this statement? Why or why not?

3. Which of the uses of insects mentioned in Listening Two might be interesting to Dr. Solomon? Why?

5 REVIEWING LANGUAGE

A. EXPLORING LANGUAGE: Plural *S*

There are three different pronunciations for the plural *s*.

1. /s/ After the voiceless sounds /p/, /t/, /k/, and /θ/

   Example: ant → ants

2. /z/ After the voiced sounds /b/, /d/, /g/, /v/, /m/, /n/, /ŋ/, /l/, /r/ and after vowel sounds

   Examples: spider → spiders
   firefly → fireflies

3. /iz/ After /s/, /z/, /ʃ/, /ʒ/, /tʃ/ and /dʒ/

   Example: cockroach → cockroaches

Note: /θ/ is the sound in *mo<u>th</u>*. /ʃ/ is the sound in *<u>fish</u>*. /ʒ/ is the sound in *beige*. /tʃ/ is the sound in *lun<u>ch</u>*. /dʒ/ is the sound in *college*.

1 *Listen to the names of the insects. Write the names under the correct column in the box.*

ants   fireflies   maggots

butterflies   praying mantises   mosquitoes

crickets   bees   spiders

cockroaches   ladybugs   termites

/S/	/Z/	/IZ/
ants	spiders	cockroaches

Listen again and repeat the names. Practice the three pronunciations of the plural **s**.

2 *Work in pairs. Look at the descriptions of insects. Choose one description, but don't tell your partner. Think of all the insects from the list that fit the description. Tell your partner the names of the insects. Be sure to use the plural form, with correct pronunciation. Your partner will guess the description and say the whole sentence.*

Example

Student A: Butterflies, bees, fireflies, and mosquitoes.

Student B: Butterflies, bees, fireflies, and mosquitoes <u>can fly</u>.

Descriptions

Are beautiful   Can fly

Are dangerous for people   Can jump

Are disgusting   Can walk

Are useful to people   Live in houses

Bite people

B. WORKING WITH WORDS

1 *The examples below show relationships between words. Here are three types of relationships.*

Cause : Effect Shows the result of an action.	**Study : Learn** If you **study,** you will **learn** something.
Opposite Shows two opposite things.	**Remember : Forget** The opposite of **remember** is **forget**.
Part : Whole Shows a small part of something larger.	**Book : Library** A **book** is part of a **library**. [or] A **novel** is a kind of **book.**

Work with a partner. Choose the correct word below to complete each word relationship. Then write an explanation like the example sentences above. The first one has been done for you.

Cause : Effect (If . . .)   **Explanation**

1. poison : _____ *die* _____   *If you take poison, you will die.*

    live   eat   die

2. train : _____   _____

    learn   teach   forget

3. do an experiment : _____   _____

    be a failure   find out   remember

Opposite (The opposite of . . .)

4. success : _____   _____

   sadness happiness failure

5. smart : _____   _____

   intelligent stupid crazy

6. get rid of : _____   _____

   throw away kill keep

Part : Whole (_____ is part of . . .) or (_____ is a kind of . . .)

7. cockroach : _____   _____

   insect animal fish

8. apartment : _____   _____

   city building room

9. biology : _____   _____

   study chemistry science

❷ *Read the following word pairs with your partner. Decide what type of relationship is presented. Write each word pair in the correct column. The first one has been done for you.*

~~person : generation~~	fly swatter : extermination method
breed : babies	predictable : unpredictable
advantage : disadvantage	dangerous : safe
apple : fruit	exterminate : die
pick up : put down	kitchen : house
feed : live	collect : together

Cause : Effect	Opposite	Part : Whole
1.	1.	1. person : generation
2.	2.	2.
3.	3.	3.
4.	4.	4.

6 GRAMMAR AND STYLE

A. GRAMMAR: Infinitives of Purpose

❶ *Read the following conversation. Notice the infinitives of purpose. Then answer the questions below.*

REPORTER: Why did you put out insect traps?

DR. SOLOMON: I put out the insect traps *to kill* the cockroaches.

REPORTER: But you didn't put out any poison.

DR. SOLOMON: No, I used the insect traps *in order not to get* poison in my food.

REPORTER: Then later you decided to breed the cockroaches. Why was that?

DR. SOLOMON: *To train* them to do things.

1. What word comes before the verb in an infinitive?

2. What form does the verb take in an infinitive?

3. Which one of the following questions does an infinitive of purpose answer: *Who? What? When? Where? Why?* or *How?*

FOCUS ON GRAMMAR

See Infinitives of Purpose in *Focus on Grammar, Intermediate.*

Infinitives of Purpose

a. To explain the purpose of an action: ◆ Use an **infinitive** ◆ Use *in order* + **infinitive**	I put the cockroaches in a jar **to kill** the cockroaches. I used insect traps **in order to kill** the cockroaches.
b. To explain a negative purpose: ◆ Use *in order not* + **infinitive**	I used insect traps **in order not to get** poison in my food.
c. To answer the question *Why?*: ◆ Use an **infinitive**	**Why** did you do that? **To kill** the cockroaches.

❷ *Match the following actions with the reasons for the actions. Then combine the two sentences into one sentence, using an infinitive of purpose. Write the sentences on the lines below. The first one has been done for you.*

Action

_b_ 1. Dr. Solomon used insect traps.

_____ 2. He used a fly swatter.

_____ 3. He went to the park in the springtime.

_____ 4. He opened his window at night.

_____ 5. He put some cream on his arms.

_____ 6. He cleaned the corner of his ceiling.

_____ 7. He cleaned all the food off the kitchen table.

_____ 8. He put some ladybugs in his garden.

_____ 9. He kept a hive full of bees in the garden.

Reason

a. He didn't want to get mosquito bites.

b. He wanted to get rid of the cockroaches.

c. He didn't want to have any spider webs.

d. He didn't want to leave any food for the ants.

e. He wanted to get rid of the flies.

f. He wanted to stop other insects from eating his plants.

g. He wanted to hear the crickets singing.

h. He wanted to make honey.

i. He wanted to see the butterflies.

1. Dr. Solomon used insect traps to get rid of the cockroaches.

2. _____

3. _____

4. _____

5. _____

6. _____

7. _____

8. _____

9. _____

❸ *Work in pairs. Student A asks a question. Student B answers using an infinitive of purpose. If you don't know the answer to a question, think of a funny answer. Switch roles after item 5. Then compare your answers with another pair of students.*

1. Why do bees make honey?

2. Why do crickets sing?

3. Why do butterflies have beautiful colors?

4. Why do ants walk in a line?

5. Why do mosquitoes drink our blood?

6. Why do spiders make spider webs?

7. Why do bees sting people?

8. Why do fireflies have light coming from their bodies?

9. Why do ants live inside our houses?

10. Why do ladybugs have spots?

B. STYLE: Agreeing and Disagreeing

When you have a discussion, it is important to know how to agree and disagree in a polite way.

STUDENT A: I think honeybees are very useful insects. They make honey for us.

STUDENT B: *That's a good point.* They also help the flowers grow into fruit.

STUDENT A: But I don't like termites. I think they're disgusting.

STUDENT B: *I'm not sure I agree with you.* They're actually a very good source of food. People in some countries eat them.

STUDENT A: Really? I didn't know that.

Agreement	Disagreement
That's a good point.	I'm sorry, but I have to disagree.
I see your point.	I'm not sure I agree with you.
That's right.	Yes, but . . .
I agree.	I disagree.
	Note: It is usually very rude to say, "You're wrong," when you disagree with someone.

Work in pairs. Student A reads each statement. Student B agrees or disagrees with the statement by choosing an expression from the box above. If you disagree, explain why. Switch roles after item 5.

Example

STUDENT A: Bees are very friendly insects.

STUDENT B: *I'm sorry, but I have to disagree.*
They'll sting you if you get too close!

1. Bees are very friendly.

2. Most people like cockroaches.

3. Butterflies are usually colorful.

4. Mosquitoes are annoying.

5. It's useful to have termites in your house.

6. Crickets make a nice sound at night.

7. Ladybugs are sometimes harmful to plants.

8. It's difficult to kill ants that live in your house.

9. Maggots are dangerous for your health.

10. It's nice to find a fly in your soup.

7 ON YOUR OWN

A. SPEAKING TOPIC: Evaluating New Uses of Insects and Other Bugs

Imagine you are part of an international scientific group. Your group gives money to scientists to develop new technology. Scientists give you a description of their work, and you must decide who will get the money. You must choose the project that will be the most useful for everyone in the world. As you discuss, remember to use the language for agreeing and disagreeing (see Section 6B).

a. Read about each proposal.

b. Work in a small group. Evaluate each proposal by answering these questions:

  ◆ Why is this technology important?

  ◆ Is the technology useful to most people in the world or only to a few people?

  ◆ How will the technology help people?

  ◆ What new problems will the technology cause?

c. Decide which project will get the money.

d. Tell the class what you decided and why.

Proposal 1: New Insect Group

Problem: Insects eat the crops that farmers grow in the fields. Over the years farmers have had to use stronger and stronger insecticides to kill insects. Many of the poisons used to kill the insects today cannot be used safely anymore because they are harmful to people. We need a new way to control the insects. If we don't find a new way, people will start getting sick from all the poisons that they are eating.

Solution: Breed new insects that will eat the insects that harm farmers' plants.

Proposal 2: Spiderweb Group

Problem: With all the new telephone and computer communication, we need new cables to connect the machines all over the world. We need a new material that is light, flexible, and strong. This new material can be used to make cables that can connect computers and telephones around the world. If we don't find a new material for cables, we will have problems with international communications.

Solution: Study spiderwebs—which are very light, flexible, and strong—in order to learn how to develop a new type of cable.

Proposal 3: Insect Medicine Group

Problem: There are many diseases, such as cancer, that doctors do not know how to cure completely. We need new medicines to help people who have deadly diseases. If we don't find new cures, people will continue to die of these diseases.

Solution: Some insects make chemicals in their bodies that we can use to make medicine. Scientists need to study different insects in order to find new medicines.

Recommendation: _____

Reasons: _____

_____

_____

B. FIELDWORK

1. SURVEY

Ask five people (not from your class) how they feel about insects. Find out the following:

* *An insect people like and why*
* *An insect that people dislike and why*
* *An insect people are afraid of and why*

Complete the chart on page 76. Then look at the results and decide which are the most popular and least popular insects. Compare your results with those of your classmates.

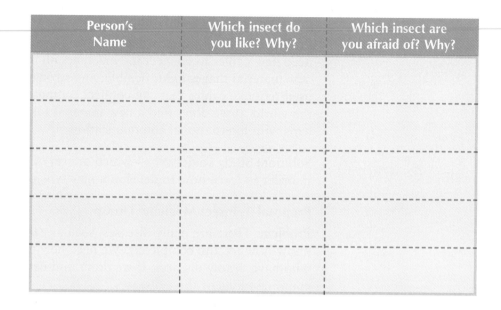

Person's Name	Which insect do you like? Why?	Which insect are you afraid of? Why?

2. RESEARCH PROJECT AND PRESENTATION

Choose an insect that you would like to know more about. Some examples of interesting insects are army ants, assassin bugs, cicadas, dragonflies, dung beetles, fruit flies, seventeen-year locusts, tsetse flies, and water bugs. If you need some other ideas, look at the pictures at the beginning of the unit. Go to the library and look up the insect in an encyclopedia or on the Internet. Find out the following information and make a short presentation to your class about the insect.

a. Where does the insect live?

b. What does the insect eat?

c. What types of insects or animals eat the insect?

d. Is there anything unusual or interesting about the insect?

e. How is the insect harmful or helpful to people?

Listening Task

Take notes on your classmates' presentations. Choose one presentation that you thought was interesting and write a paragraph explaining the information you heard.

UNDERSTANDING ACCENTS

1 APPROACHING THE TOPIC

A. PREDICTING

Read the cartoon and discuss these questions with the class.

1. What are the two men doing?
2. Where are they from?
3. How does each man feel about the other?
4. What do you think this unit will be about?

B. SHARING INFORMATION

Sometimes people who speak the same language have different pronunciations or accents. They may even have different words for the same things. For example, in English the word for what you put your groceries in at the supermarket can be *wagon, buggy,* or *cart.*

❶ *Think of different accents that you hear when people speak your native language. Read the statements. Write* **A** *if you agree with the statement and* **D** *if you disagree. Discuss your answers in a small group.*

1. In my native language, you can tell the following things by listening to someone's accent:

    _____ Where the person is from

    _____ Whether a person is rich or poor

    _____ The person's level of education

2. _____ In my native language, some accents are considered to be better than others.

3. _____ In my native language, I can understand everybody's accent.

❷ *What do you usually do when you can't understand someone's accent in your native language? Check (✓) all the strategies you use. If you use a different strategy from the ones listed, write it in the blank. Discuss your answers in a small group.*

    _____ 1. Tell the person that you don't understand

    _____ 2. Ask the person to repeat what was said

    _____ 3. Pretend that you understand

    _____ 4. Try to end the conversation quickly

    _____ 5. [other] _____

    _____ 6. [other] _____

❸ *What do you usually do when you can't understand someone's accent* **in English?** *Look at the strategies in Exercise 2. Underline all the strategies you use. If you use a different strategy from the ones listed, write it in the blank. Discuss your answers in a small group.*

2 PREPARING TO LISTEN

A. BACKGROUND

How do you feel about your pronunciation in English? Check your opinions in the chart below. Check SA (strongly agree), A (agree), D (disagree), or SD (strongly disagree). Then compare your answers with those of a partner.

YOUR OPINION	SA	A	D	SD
1. I feel uncomfortable speaking in English because of my accent.				
2. I will learn incorrect pronunciation if my classmates speak incorrect English.				
3. It is possible for me to improve my English pronunciation.				
4. It is possible for me to have perfect English pronunciation someday.				
5. Pronunciation classes can help me to speak English more clearly.				
6. Living in an English-speaking country can help me to improve my pronunciation.				
7. Listening to a lot of English can help me to improve my pronunciation.				
8. British English is more correct than American English.				
9. It's important to have perfect pronunciation in English.				
10. People will be able to understand me even if I speak English with an accent.				

B. VOCABULARY FOR COMPREHENSION

1 *Read the paragraphs. Guess the meanings of the underlined words.*

LEARNING ENGLISH

It isn't easy for adult students of English to improve their accents. Unlike children, who are (**1**) <u>flexible</u>, adults often find it hard to change the way they speak. This is why even the (**2**) <u>top</u>, or smartest, adult students have difficulty with pronunciation.

There are several things that an international student can do to improve his or her pronunciation. One method is to (**3**) <u>sign up</u> for a pronunciation class. Studying pronunciation can help students to understand the rules of English, but in order to practice speaking, students often need to (**4**) <u>be exposed to</u> English outside the classroom as well. This is why many students say that studying in an English-speaking country greatly (**5**) <u>affects</u> their English. Living with native speakers can help students to (**6**) <u>pick up</u> new vocabulary as well as improve their accents. International students can also learn important cultural information. This can help to prevent (**7**) <u>misunderstandings</u> that can occur when people from different cultures live together.

Living with someone from another culture can be difficult. International students are usually excited when they first (**8**) <u>show up</u> at their new homes, but after a few months they may start to think about their home countries and get (**9**) <u>homesick</u>. Students who are homesick get (**10**) <u>depressed</u> easily. They might cry a lot or want to be alone. This makes it difficult for them to make friends and learn English.

2 *Below are the definitions of the underlined words. Write the number of the word that corresponds to each definition. The first one has been done for you. Compare your answers with those of a partner.*

_____ **a.** to learn

_____ **b.** the best

__1__ **c.** easy to change

_____ **d.** produces a change

_____ **e.** have experiences with

_____ **f.** how you feel when you miss your home

_____ **g.** problems with communication

_____ **h.** agree to participate in

_____ **i.** arrive

_____ **j.** sad

3 | LISTENING ONE: | Understanding Accents

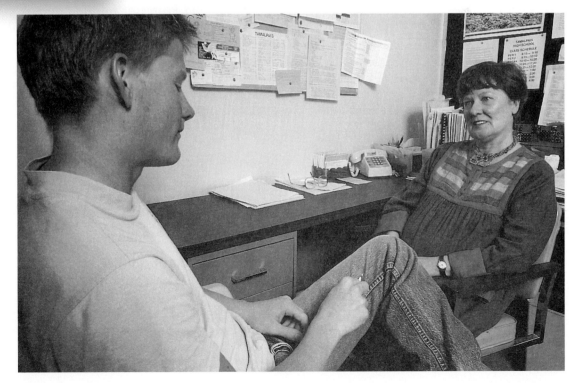

A. INTRODUCING THE TOPIC

Listen to the first part of the conversation between a student and a professor. Write answers to the questions.

1. Where does this conversation take place?

_____

2. Where is the student from? How do you know?

_____

3. Where is the professor from? How do you know?

_____

4. What do you think the conversation will be about?

_____

B. LISTENING FOR MAIN IDEAS

In their conversation, Fredrick and Professor Johnson discuss many topics about language learning and accents. Read the topics below. Listen to the whole conversation. Number the topics from 1 to 6 in the order that you hear them. The first one has been done for you.

Fredrick and Professor Johnson discuss:

_____ if Fredrick should take a pronunciation class

__1__ if Fredrick will learn incorrect pronunciation from his classmates

_____ misunderstandings caused by incorrect pronunciation

_____ the best type of English accent to learn

_____ the difference between adult and child language learners

_____ places where Fredrick hears American English

C. LISTENING FOR DETAILS

Read the statements. Listen to the conversation again. Circle the answer that best completes each sentence.

1. Fredrick and Professor Johnson _____.

   a. have never met   **b.** met in class last semester

2. Professor Johnson tells Fredrick that students _____ learn their classmates' accents.

   a. don't usually   **b.** usually

3. Children _____ the same accents as their mothers.

   a. always have   **b.** don't always have

4. Most adult language learners _____ their accents.

   a. can lose   **b.** never lose

5. Fredrick wonders if he should take a _____ class next semester.

   a. pronunciation   **b.** conversation

6. Sylvia was _____.

   a. homesick for her country   **b.** at home with a bad cold

7. The student who said "homesick" used the wrong _____.

   a. stress   **b.** intonation

8. Professor Johnson speaks with Indian, British, and _____ accents.

   a. Australian   **b.** South African

9. Professor Johnson thinks that _____.

   a. a British accent is better than an American accent   **b.** no accent is better than another accent

10. At the end, Fredrick decides _____.

    a. to take a pronunciation class   **b.** to wait to make a decision about a pronunciation class

D. LISTENING BETWEEN THE LINES

During her conversation with Fredrick, Professor Johnson tries to persuade him not to worry so much about his accent. Does Fredrick believe her? Listen to these excerpts from the listening. After each excerpt decide if Fredrick is persuaded by Professor Johnson's explanation. Check (✓) your opinion and write the reason for your answer. Discuss your answers with the class.

	FREDRICK'S FEELINGS			REASON FOR YOUR ANSWER
	Persuaded	**Somewhat Persuaded**	**Not Persuaded**	
Excerpt 1				
Excerpt 2				
Excerpt 3				
Excerpt 4				
Excerpt 5				

4 LISTENING TWO: Accents and Children

A. EXPANDING THE TOPIC

Listen to the excerpt from a lecture about accents and language learning in children. Answer the questions by circling the correct choice.

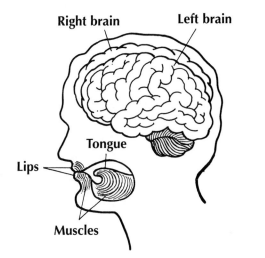

1. The professor says that children learn languages _____ than adults.

   a. more easily   **b.** less easily

2. The muscles in children's mouths are _____. This allows them to make new sounds easily.

   a. long   **b.** flexible

3. There are two sides to an adult brain, and each side helps us to _____.

   a. do different things   **b.** think through problems

4. A child's brain is _____.

   a. divided into a left and a   **b.** not yet divided into a left and
   right side   a right side

B. LINKING LISTENINGS ONE AND TWO

① *Look at the chart that you completed earlier on page 79.*

1. Now think about Professor Johnson's opinions. Answer the questions the way she would answer them.

2. Compare your answers in a small group. Do you agree on the responses? Do you disagree on any?

3. Have you changed any of your opinions as a result of the listening? Why or why not? Discuss your observations with a partner.

② *Do you understand the explanations given in Listening Two? Work with a partner. Student A summarizes how muscle differences might affect how children learn accents. Student B summarizes how brain differences might affect how children learn accents. Are your partner's explanations correct? Discuss any differences of opinion.*

③ *In Listenings One and Two the professors talk about differences between child and adult language learning. Do you agree with their opinions? Can you think of any other reasons for the differences? Discuss these questions in pairs or small groups.*

5 REVIEWING LANGUAGE

A. EXPLORING LANGUAGE: Question Intonation

Question Intonation

Yes/No Questions Use Rising Intonation

Yes/no questions end with rising intonation. Your voice goes up and gets higher at the end of the question.

◆ Can I talk with you for a minute?

Wh- Questions Use Falling Intonation

Wh- questions end with falling intonation. Your voice gets lower at the end of the question.

◆ What can I do for you?

It is important to use correct *intonation* in asking questions.

1 *Listen to the conversation. Mark the correct intonation at the end of each question. Use arrows (_____↗ or ‾‾‾↘). Now work with a partner. Compare your intonation markings. Then read the conversation aloud. One partner takes the role of Kimiko and the other of the professor. Then switch roles and read the conversation again.*

KIMIKO: Professor Brown. (**1**) Do you have a minute?

PROFESSOR: Yes. (**2**) How can I help you? (**3**) Are you having a problem in class?

KIMIKO: Oh no! I enjoy your class, but it only meets three hours a week. (**4**) How can I get more English?

PROFESSOR: Well, you could listen to English news programs on the radio.

KIMIKO: That's a good idea!

PROFESSOR: You could also watch English-language movies. (**5**) What kinds of movies do you like?

KIMIKO: I like comedies. You're right, I should watch more movies. These are good suggestions for listening. (**6**) Do you have any suggestions for speaking?

PROFESSOR: (**7**) Could you take a pronunciation class? Professor Price is teaching one this semester. (**8**) Do you know him?

KIMIKO: Yes, I do! (**9**) When does the class meet?

PROFESSOR: I'm not sure. You'd better ask him.

KIMIKO: I'll do that right now. Thanks for your advice.

PROFESSOR: You're welcome!

② *Work with a partner. Complete the questions in the conversation below. Then mark the intonation of each question with arrows. Now read the conversation aloud. One partner takes the role of Kimiko and the other of the professor. Switch roles and read the conversations again.*

KIMIKO: Excuse me Professor Price. **(1)** Do you

_____?

PROFESSOR: Yes, I have some time. **(2)** How can I

_____?

KIMIKO: I need to get some information about your

pronunciation class. **(3)** When _____?

PROFESSOR: We meet on Mondays, Wednesdays, and Fridays.

KIMIKO: **(4)** And what _____?

PROFESSOR: It's at 9:00 A.M.

KIMIKO: **(5)** Can I _____?

PROFESSOR: Yes, you can still sign up. I have three spaces left.

(6) Do you _____?

KIMIKO: No, I don't have any more questions. Thanks for your help!

PROFESSOR: You're welcome!

B. WORKING WITH WORDS: Phrasal Verbs

A **phrasal verb** is a two-part verb that has a special meaning.

Phrasal Verbs

A **phrasal verb** contains **a verb + a particle** (a preposition or an adverb). A phrasal verb has a different meaning from the meaning of the verb itself.

◆ Fredrick **stopped by** Professor Johnson's office.

stopped by = visited
(verb + particle)

1 *Read the sentences. Guess the meanings of the underlined phrasal verbs. Write the letters of the answers in the blanks.*

1. _____ I <u>pick up</u> languages very easily. I speak Cantonese, Thai, and English.

   _____ I need to <u>pick out</u> an English class to take. Which one should I take?

   a. choose   **b.** learn

2. _____ I speak French to my children. When my children <u>grow up</u>, I hope they will speak French to their children.

   _____ My daughter will <u>grow out of</u> those shoes very quickly. I'd better get the next size.

   a. become adults   **b.** become too big for

3. _____ Please <u>sign in</u> on this piece of paper so that I know you're here.

   _____ I want to <u>sign up for</u> the class, but it's already full.

   a. become part of   **b.** write your name when you arrive

4. _____ The professor likes students to participate. That's why she <u>calls on</u> them in class.

   _____ The professor will <u>call off</u> the test if the students aren't prepared.

   a. cancel   **b.** asks to speak

5. _____ That student likes to <u>show off</u>. She talks all the time.

   _____ The professor likes her students to <u>show up</u> to class on time.

   a. arrive   **b.** try to get people to notice her

6. _____ I don't like the title of my paper. I need to <u>think up</u> another one.

   _____ I need to <u>think over</u> your advice before I make a decision.

   a. consider carefully   **b.** create a new idea for

7. _____ I'll <u>drop by</u> Joe's house to talk about the assignment. He's a good friend, so I don't have to call before I arrive.

   _____ I've decided to <u>drop out of</u> school. I don't want to leave, but my life is too busy at the moment.

   a. informally visit   **b.** quit

② *Work with a partner. Read these sentences from the listening. The verb is given but the particle is missing. Fill in the blank with a particle from the list. Some particles can be used more than once and some are not used at all.*

over   by   off   up   on   in   out   out of

1. There's no way you can pick _____up_____ a different accent just from being in class a few hours a week.

2. Say you have a mother from Germany living in the United States. . . . Even if the mother speaks English with a German accent, her child will still grow _____ speaking American English.

3. That makes me wonder about if I should take that pronunciation class that I signed _____ for next semester.

4. Today, when I was calling _____ students in my speaking class, I noticed that one of my students was absent.

5. I asked the class why Sylvia hadn't shown _____.

6. I have to check _____ a book from the library before class, so I'd better get going.

7. Thanks for your advice. I'll think _____ what you said.

8. Have a good semester and drop _____ any time!

③ *With a partner write a short conversation about education in your country. Include as many phrasal verbs from Exercises 1 and 2 as you can. Perform your conversation for the class.*

Listening Task
As you listen to your classmates' performances, write down the phrasal verbs that you hear.

6 SKILLS FOR EXPRESSION

A. GRAMMAR: Modals and Related Verbs of Advice

1 *Kimiko wrote to her friend Ken to tell him about her conversation with Professor Brown. Read the letter. Notice the boldfaced words. They express advice. Then answer the questions below.*

> Dear Ken,
>
> I talked with Professor Brown as you suggested. He said that I **should** listen to the radio and watch English-language movies. He also thinks I **ought to** study pronunciation. The class is popular, so I **shouldn't** wait too long to sign up. In fact, I **'d better** sign up today. Well, I **'d better not** waste any more time or I'll miss my bus. Thanks for your advice.
>
> Kimiko

1. What are the modals or other verbs of advice in the letter?

2. What are the differences in meaning among these expressions?

FOCUS ON GRAMMAR

See Modals and Related Verbs
of Advice in *Focus on
Grammar, Intermediate.*

Modals and Related Verbs of Advice

a. To ask for advice, use **should.**

Should I study pronunciation?
What **should** I study?

b. To give advice, use . . .

◆ **should**

He **should** study pronunciation.

◆ **should not** (**shouldn't**)

He **should not** (**shouldn't**) study
pronunciation.

◆ **ought to**

He **ought to** study pronunciation.

Note: **Ought to** is generally not used
with a negative in American English.

c. To give strong advice, use . . .

◆ **had better** (**'d better**)

He **had better** (**'d better**) study
pronunciation.

◆ **had better not** (**'d better not**)

He **had better not** (**'d better not**)
study pronunciation.

Note: The verb that follows *should,
ought to,* and *had better* always
takes the base form.

---

2 *Work in groups of four. Student A will ask for advice. The other
three students will give Student A advice, using **should, shouldn't,
ought to, had better,** or **had better not.** Then Student B will ask for
advice. Continue in this way, using the items in the list below.*

Example

STUDENT A: I always sleep late and miss my morning class. What
should I do?

STUDENT B: You *shouldn't* go to bed so late.

STUDENT C: You *ought to* ask your roommate to wake you up.

STUDENT D: You*'d better* buy a new alarm clock.

1. I want to make friends with some native speakers of English.

2. I want to study at an American university, but my TOEFL score
is too low.

3. I want to study English, but my family wants me to study
engineering.

4. I'm going to Australia for a vacation, so I want to learn some
Australian slang.

5. I want to have a party for the students in my class, but my
apartment is too small.

6. I want to buy a present for the students in my class, but I don't know what to get.

7. I'm in love with one of the students in my class, but he/she doesn't know it.

8. My friend wants me to write his English paper for him, but I think that's cheating.

B. STYLE: Starting a Conversation

Fredrick begins his conversation with Professor Johnson by saying, "Do you have a minute?" This is a polite way to start a conversation. Here are some other ways to start a conversation.

Conversation Openers

- Do you have a minute?
- Can I talk with you for a minute?
- Can you help me?
- Are you busy?
- May I ask you something?
- Are you free?

Responses to Conversation Openers

There are different ways to respond to a polite opener.

If you want to talk, you can say:	If you don't want to talk, you can say:
• Sure!	• Sorry, I'm busy.
• Yes! How can I help you?	• Sorry, I have to _____.

Work in two groups, A and B. Walk around the classroom.

Group A Students

Ask some Group B students the questions below. Before asking the questions, use polite language to start the conversation. Ask questions for ten minutes.

1. What is your native language?

2. What other languages do you speak?

3. Why are you studying English?

Group B Students

When the first Group A student asks to speak with you, politely accept and answer the survey questions. When the next Group A student asks to speak with you, politely refuse. Continue to take turns accepting and refusing until Group A students have finished their survey. Answer questions for ten minutes.

Example

STUDENT A: Do you have a minute?

STUDENT B: Sure!

STUDENT A: I'd like to ask you a few questions . . .

[or]

STUDENT A: Do you have a minute?

STUDENT B: Sorry, I'm busy.

STUDENT A: OK . . .

Now switch. Group B students ask the survey questions. Group A students answer.

7 ON YOUR OWN

A. SPEAKING TOPICS: Role Play

Part A

Here are some problems that students of English often have. Read these problems in pairs. Think of at least three solutions to each problem.

a. "It's hard for me to understand my classmates, especially during group work, so I don't feel like talking."

b. "My classmates are so quiet. I want to have good discussions, but they don't want to say anything. I feel as if I'm the only person who is answering questions."

c. "I only hear English three hours a week during class. I think that's not enough to really learn."

d. "My classmates often speak their own languages during class. It wastes everyone's time. I think we should only speak English."

e. "I'm embarrassed about my pronunciation. That's why I'm so quiet in class. I want to speak more, but I'm too shy."

Part B

With your partner, choose one of the problems above. Create a conversation between a professor and a student. The student will explain his/her problem and the professor will give three suggestions for how to solve the problem.

a. Choose a problem and decide where the conversation will take place.

b. Decide who will be the student and who will be the professor.

c. Plan and practice a conversation. (Don't write it out.) (Use the language for giving advice [see Section 6A] and starting a conversation [see Section 6B].)

d. Perform the conversation for your classmates. (Use correct question intonation [see Section 5A].)

Listening Task

As your classmates perform, write answers to the following questions.

a. What is the student's problem?

b. What three suggestions does the professor give?

c. What do you think of the professor's suggestions?

B. FIELDWORK

SURVEY

Conduct a survey on people's feelings about accents.

a. Work in a small group.

b. Choose survey 1, 2, or 3 on the page 96. Look at the survey questions with your group. Add one question.

c. With a partner from your group, go outside class and ask four people the questions. (Use conversation starters.)

d. Return to your group and report your findings.

e. Use the information you gathered to prepare a group presentation for the class.

Survey 1: Accents and Conversations

Do you have trouble understanding some English accents? If so, which ones?

If you're talking with someone and you can't understand their accent, what do you do?

_____

_____ ?

Survey 2: Accents and Attitudes

Is a British accent better than an American accent? If so, why? If not, why not?

Can you tell how much education a person has by listening to his/her accent? Why/why not?

_____

_____ ?

Survey 3: Accents and Language Learning

Is it possible for an adult to change his/her accent? If so, how? If not, why not?

Is it important for international students of English to lose their accents? Why/why not?

_____

_____ ?

WORKING WITH AIDS PATIENTS

1 APPROACHING THE TOPIC

A. PREDICTING

Look at the picture of a healthcare worker. Read the title of the unit. Discuss these questions with the class.

1. Why does the healthcare worker need to wear special clothing?

2. What difficulties do you think healthcare workers have when they work with patients who have AIDS?

B. SHARING INFORMATION

Discuss these questions in a small group.

1. Can you tell by looking at someone if the person has AIDS or HIV? Why or why not?

2. Would you take a job or volunteer to work with people who have AIDS? Why or why not?

3. Although AIDS and cancer are both deadly diseases, many people feel sorry for cancer patients but not for AIDS patients. What do you think is the reason for this?

PREPARING TO LISTEN

A. BACKGROUND

1 *Read the paragraph.*

AIDS (Acquired Immunodeficiency Syndrome) is one of the world's greatest health problems. Since 1981, when AIDS was first identified in the United States, millions of people all over the world have died from the disease. AIDS is caused by a virus that weakens people so much that they become sick. The name of the virus is HIV (Human Immunodeficiency Virus). The most common ways of getting HIV are through having sex with a person who has HIV, using dirty needles to take drugs, receiving blood from a person who has HIV, and passing the virus from mother to baby. In a few situations, healthcare workers, such as doctors and nurses, have gotten the virus from the blood of patients with HIV.

2 *Can a healthcare worker get HIV from a patient with AIDS? Read the statements and check your opinions below. Then discuss your opinions with the class.*

AN AIDS QUIZ

Can you get HIV by . . .	Yes	Maybe	No
1. being in the same room as an AIDS patient?	❏	❏	❏
2. breathing after a patient coughs?	❏	❏	❏
3. holding a patient's hand?	❏	❏	❏
4. giving a patient some pills?	❏	❏	❏
5. touching a patient's blood?	❏	❏	❏
6. touching the sheets on a patient's bed?	❏	❏	❏
7. touching a patient's tears?	❏	❏	❏
8. taking a patient's temperature?	❏	❏	❏
9. giving an injection to a patient?	❏	❏	❏
10. breathing into a patient's mouth during an emergency?	❏	❏	❏

B. VOCABULARY FOR COMPREHENSION

Read the conversations. Then choose the best words to complete the definitions of the underlined words.

1. A: Does she work in the children's <u>ward</u> of the hospital?
   B: No, she works in the AIDS ward.

   A <u>ward</u> is a _____ in a hospital.

   a. department   **b.** healthcare worker

2. A: How do people get colds?
   B: Usually they <u>get infected</u> by being around someone else who is sick.

   To get <u>infected</u> means to get a _____ inside the body.

   a. pain   **b.** disease

3. A: Is there a <u>risk</u> of getting a disease from a patient in the hospital?
   B: Yes, there's a small chance, but it doesn't usually happen if you follow the safety rules.

   A <u>risk</u> means it is _____ for something to happen.

   a. not possible   **b.** possible

4. A: Why is the doctor wearing paper clothing and plastic glasses?
   B: That's <u>protective</u> clothing. She's wearing it so she won't get a disease from the patient.

   <u>Protective</u> clothing helps keep a person _____ by covering the person's skin.

   a. safe   **b.** strong

5. A: That doctor is always very polite to his patients.
   B: Yes, he thinks it is important to <u>treat them with respect</u>.

   To <u>treat someone with respect</u> means to make people feel

   _____.

   a. healthy   **b.** that you care about them

6. A: You can't get AIDS from just breathing the air in a patient's room.
   B: Oh. So that's why you don't need to <u>isolate</u> AIDS patients in separate rooms.

   To <u>isolate</u> means to keep people _____.

   a. apart   **b.** busy

7. A: The AIDS virus lives in people's <u>bodily fluids</u>, so you should be careful not to touch a patient's blood.
   B: I'm glad you told me.

   <u>Bodily fluids</u> are liquids that _____ a person's body.

   a. come from   **b.** touch

8. A: How did you burn your hand?
   B: I was working in a laboratory in the hospital, and my hand <u>came in contact with</u> a chemical that burned me.

   To <u>come in contact with</u> something means to _____ something.

   a. touch   **b.** stay away from

9. A: Did you <u>draw the patient's blood</u>?
   B: Yes. I only took a small amount. It's in that bottle over there.

   To <u>draw someone's blood</u> means to _____ someone's blood.

   a. draw a picture of   **b.** take out

10. A: I'm afraid that I might <u>prick</u> my finger while I'm giving a patient an injection.
    B: It's possible. To be safe you should always wear gloves.

    To <u>prick</u> yourself means to cut yourself with a _____.

    a. knife   **b.** needle

11. A: Always be honest with your patients. That's what my advisor told me to do.
    B: That's a good <u>rule to live by</u>. I always try to tell my patients the truth.

    A <u>rule to live by</u> is an idea to _____.

    a. remember   **b.** ignore

12. A: Is there a <u>cure</u> for AIDS?
    B: Not yet. We can't remove the virus from the body, but we can help people feel healthier.

    To <u>cure</u> a disease means to make it _____.

    a. slow down   **b.** go away completely

LISTENING ONE: Training a Nurse's Assistant

A. INTRODUCING THE TOPIC

You will hear a conversation between two nurses. Listen to the beginning of the conversation. Answer the questions.

1. Where is the conversation taking place?

2. Which of the two nurses has more experience, Nicky or Susan?

3. Nicky is worried. What do you think she is worried about?

B. LISTENING FOR MAIN IDEAS

Listen to the conversation. Circle the best answer to complete each sentence. Compare your answers with a partner.

1. Nicky is worried about _____ with HIV.

    a. becoming infected   **b.** being infected now   **c.** knowing someone infected

2. Nicky's family has _____ about her new job.

    a. no worries   **b.** good feelings   **c.** bad feelings

3. Susan says that it's important _____ AIDS patients.

    a. not to isolate   **b.** to completely isolate   **c.** to carefully watch

4. Susan tells Nicky that AIDS can be passed through _____.

    a. serving lunch to a patient   **b.** sharing bodily fluids   **c.** giving blood to a patient

5. Susan thinks that Nicky should wear protective clothing _____.

    a. whenever she   **b.** only sometimes   **c.** all day at the
    sees a patient   hospital

6. Susan's patients on the AIDS ward _____.

    a. sometimes get   **b.** are always sad   **c.** sometimes
    cured   become healthy

C. LISTENING FOR DETAILS

*Listen to the conversation again. Read each statement and decide if it is true or false. Write **T** or **F**. Compare your answers with those of a partner.*

_____ **1.** Susan is Nicky's advisor.

_____ **2.** There is a high risk of getting infected with HIV at work.

_____ **3.** Susan lost some friends when she started working on the AIDS ward.

_____ **4.** Nicky's patient was angry when she wore protective clothing to bring him lunch.

_____ **5.** Susan says that patients need to be treated with respect.

_____ **6.** Nicky says that if she had AIDS she would feel safer if her nurses wore protective clothing.

_____ **7.** It is possible to get AIDS from sharing a glass of water.

_____ **8.** When Nicky draws someone's blood, she should wear gloves.

_____ **9.** Susan sometimes feels sad working on the AIDS ward.

_____ **10.** Nicky feels more afraid after her conversation with Susan.

D. LISTENING BETWEEN THE LINES

Listen to the following excerpts. In each excerpt Susan gives Nicky one piece of advice. Does Nicky agree with the advice? Do you think she will follow it? Listen carefully to Nicky's response and circle your interpretation of her feelings. Then write a reason for your opinion. Discuss your answers with the class.

EXCERPT	WILL NICKY FOLLOW THE ADVICE?		REASON FOR YOUR OPINION
Excerpt 1	Yes	No	_____
Excerpt 2	Yes	No	_____
Excerpt 3	Yes	No	_____

LISTENING TWO: Calling an AIDS Hotline

A. EXPANDING THE TOPIC

*You will hear three phone calls to an AIDS hotline (a place you can call for information). After each phone call, choose the question the caller asks. Write **Call 1, Call 2,** or **Call 3** in the space after the correct question. Then check whether the expert says if it is possible or not possible to get AIDS.*

CAN I GET AIDS/HIV FROM . . .	THE EXPERT SAYS THAT IT IS . . .	
	possible	**not possible**
1. getting a mosquito bite? _____		
2. going to the dentist? _____		
3. kissing? _____		

B. LINKING LISTENINGS ONE AND TWO

Work in a small group. Discuss the answers to the questions.

1. Go back to the quiz you took on page 99. Do you still agree with your answers? Why or why not? Change the answers that are not correct.

2. How did the nurses in Listening One feel about AIDS patients? Do you think that most people feel that way? Why or why not?

3. People who have HIV can get information both from hospitals and from telephone hotlines. What is the difference between the services that each provides? In what situations would it be better to go to a hospital? In what situations would it be better to call an information hotline?

5 REVIEWING LANGUAGE

A. EXPLORING LANGUAGE: *Can/Can't*

It is sometimes difficult for students to hear and pronounce the difference between **can** and **can't**. Native speakers don't listen for the /t/ sound in *can't*. Instead, they listen for the length of the /a/ sound.

Listen to the example:

A: Can a mother give HIV to her baby when she's pregnant?

B: Yes, she can. She can also pass it to her baby in her milk.

A: What if she feeds the baby with a bottle?

B: She can't pass HIV by giving the baby milk in a bottle.

Can/Can't	
Can is not stressed in sentences and questions, unless it is the last word in the sentence. When it is unstressed, pronounce **can** like **kin**.	"**Kin** a mother give HIV to her baby when she's pregnant?" "Yes, she **can**."
Can't is always stressed. The vowel sound in **can't** is long. Pronounce **can't** like **kant**.	"She **kant** pass HIV through milk from a bottle, right?" "Right. She **kant**."

❶ *Listen to the following sentences. Circle* **can** *or* **can't**. *Compare your answers with those of a partner.*

1. You can/can't go in there without protective clothing.

2. The patient can/can't leave the hospital today.

3. She can/can't work this weekend.

4. Can/Can't you tell me what the problem is?

5. The doctor can/can't see you now.

6. You can/can't take an HIV test here.

7. You can/can't go in there. Yes, you can/can't.

8. These gloves can/can't protect you.

9. The hospital can/can't treat AIDS patients.

10. He can/can't understand how he got AIDS.

2 *Work in pairs. Look at the following sentences. They are the same sentences you just listened to.*

Student A: Choose **can** *or* **can't** *in each sentence and circle your choice. Then read each sentence to Student B, making sure to use the correct pronunciation. Student B will say "one" if she or he hears* **can (kin)** *and "two" if he or she hears* **can't (kant)**.

Student B: Listen to the sentences. If you hear **can (kin)**, *say "one." If you hear* **can't (kant)**, *say "two."*

After Student A completes all the sentences, switch roles.

1. You can/can't go in there without protective clothing.

2. The patient can/can't leave the hospital today.

3. She can/can't work this weekend.

4. Can/Can't you tell me what the problem is?

5. The doctor can/can't see you now.

6. You can/can't take an HIV test here.

7. We can/can't go in there.

8. These gloves can/can't protect you.

9. The hospital can/can't treat AIDS patients.

10. He can/can't understand how he got AIDS.

3 *Work in pairs. Use the information you heard in the listenings to answer these questions about how you can get HIV. For each question discuss . . .*

a. *whether you can or can't get HIV from doing the activity, and*

b. *the reasons for your answer.*

Can you get HIV by . . .

1. listening to a patient's heart?

2. having sex?

3. helping a bleeding person after an accident?

4. using someone's spoon?

5. kissing someone?

6. pricking your finger with an infected needle?

7. injecting drugs with a friend?

8. sitting in a hot tub (a bathtub with hot water) with someone?

9. shaking someone's hand?

10. getting bitten by a fly?

B. WORKING WITH WORDS: Connotations and Domains

Sometimes words can have positive or negative meanings. Words have positive meanings when they make you think of or feel something good or positive. Words have negative meanings when they make you think of or feel something bad or negative.

1 *Work in pairs. Look at the words in the list below. Divide the words into two groups. One group will go under the heading "Positive." The other group will go under the heading "Negative." You must have a reason for putting the words in each group, and you must use all the words in the list.*

AIDS	blood	bodily fluids	contact
cure	virus	respect	HIV
infected	isolate	needle	ward
protective	risk	prick	disease
	breathe	touch	

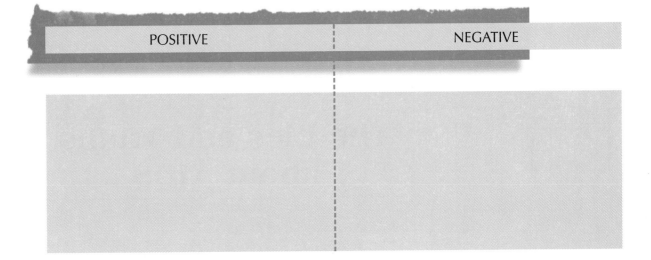

POSITIVE | NEGATIVE

Meet with another pair and compare answers. Discuss your reasons for your choices.

2 *Work with your partner again. Choose eight of the words from the list and put them in two new groups: words that make you think of a "Patient" and words that make you think of a "Healthcare Worker."*

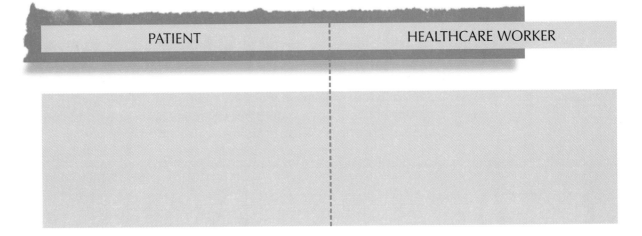

PATIENT | HEALTHCARE WORKER

6 SKILLS FOR EXPRESSION

A. GRAMMAR: *Wh-* Questions—Subject and Predicate

① *Underline the* **wh-** *question words in this advertisement for an AIDS education lecture. Then answer the questions below.*

Dr. Joseph Bleary
San Francisco General Hospital
Presenting on . . .

The Lies and Truths about AIDS

- What causes AIDS?
- How can you get infected?
- Who is at risk for getting HIV?
- When should you get tested for HIV?
- Where can you get help if you have AIDS?

Saturday, July 10th ● 7:30 P.M. ● Blakeslee Room

---

1. Why do you think this poster includes so many wh- questions?

2. *How* is a wh- question word even though it doesn't begin with *wh-*. Why is this so? What does *how* have in common with the other question words? What is another name for wh- questions?

FOCUS ON GRAMMAR

See *Wh-* Questions: Subject and Predicate in *Focus on Grammar, Intermediate.*

Wh- Questions

Use **wh-** questions to ask for specific information. Some **wh-** question words are **who(m), what, where, when, which, why,** and **how.**

a. When you ask about the subject:	Someone is at risk for AIDS.
◆ Use a **wh-** question word in place of the subject	**Who** is at risk for AIDS?
	Something causes AIDS.
	What causes AIDS?
b. When you ask about the predicate:	You can get infected somehow.
◆ Use **yes/no** question word order,	Can you get infected?
	How can you get infected?
◆ but begin with a **wh-** word	He gets AIDS tests somewhere.
	Does he get AIDS tests?
	Where does he get AIDS tests?

2 *Work in pairs. Student A, read the directions below. Student B, see Student Activities page 203.*

Student A

Read the story about a nurse who worked in an AIDS ward. Write questions on the next page to find out the missing information from your partner. (The first question is done for you.) Ask your partner the questions and fill in the information. Then answer your partner's questions.

Mary Salinger started working as a nurse in the AIDS ward at
(1) _____ on June 1, 1986. The next year, at
(2) _____ o'clock in the morning on New Year's Eve,
she saw a terrible accident while she was working in the emergency
department. While Mary was (3) _____, the doctor she
was working with accidentally pricked his hand on the bloody needle.
Three months later, the doctor took an HIV test because he found out
that the patient had AIDS. The test showed that the doctor had the
HIV virus. Mary felt (4) _____ about the accident and
the infection of the doctor. Then, two weeks later, she found out that
such accidents didn't have to happen. Another nurse told her that

there was a special type of needle that had (5) _____.
Mary thought, "This is great! We'll never have an accident with a
needle again!" She asked (6) _____ to order the safe
type of needles. He said no, he couldn't order them because they were
too expensive. Mary was very angry. She felt that saving lives was
more important than saving money.

Questions

1. _Where did Mary Salinger start working as a nurse_ ?
2. _____ ?
3. _____ ?
4. _____ ?
5. _____ ?
6. _____ ?

B. STYLE: Leading a Small Group Discussion

In a group discussion, it is useful to have a leader who helps control and
direct the conversation. The leader must know how to start and end the
discussion, how to keep the discussion on the topic, and what to do if
someone doesn't talk or talks too much.

1 *Read the phrases that you can use to help you lead a discussion.
(Don't fill in the blanks or check the boxes. They will be used for
an activity later.)*

Starting a Discussion

☐ Let's talk about . . .

☐ Today I'd like to discuss . . .

☐ _____

☐ _____

Getting Everyone to Speak

a. Asking someone to talk

☐ What do you think, [name]?

☐ [name], do you agree?

☐ _____

☐ _____

b. Asking someone to stop talking

☐ That's a good point, [name]. Can we hear from someone else?

☐ I see your point, [name]. Does anyone agree or disagree?

☐ _____

☐ _____

Staying on the Topic

☐ Let's get back to our discussion about . . .

☐ I'd like to return to the topic. What do you think about . . . ?

☐ _____

☐ _____

Ending a Discussion

☐ That's all we have time for today.

☐ To summarize, some people feel . . . , while others feel . . .
[You summarize the ideas expressed in the discussion.]

☐ _____

☐ _____

2 _Work in a small group. Choose one student to be the discussion leader and one student to be the observer. The discussion leader chooses one of the questions from the list on page 114 and leads a five-minute discussion. The observer follows these instructions:_

a. Listen quietly and fill in the checklist on pages 112–113. Check the phrases that you hear.

b. Write any additional words or phrases the discussion leader uses in the blanks.

c. Give the completed checklist to the discussion leader.

Each member of the group should have a turn as both the discussion leader and the observer.

Discussion Questions

1. Should parents teach their children about AIDS? Why or why not? If parents should teach about AIDS, when should they start talking with their children? What kinds of materials could parents use to help with their discussions?

2. Should there be AIDS education in schools? Why or why not? If there should be AIDS education in schools, which age groups should receive the information? Where else could you have AIDS education programs?

3. Should AIDS educators be allowed to communicate their message in public places like TV, billboards (large outdoor advertisements), magazines, and the Internet? Why or why not? How else could AIDS educators spread their message?

4. What topics should be discussed in AIDS education programs? What topics should not be discussed in AIDS education programs? Explain your choices.

5. Do you know about AIDS education programs in another country? If so, what kinds of programs are they? Who do the programs teach? Who pays for the programs?

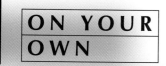

ON YOUR OWN

A. SPEAKING TOPIC: Planning an AIDS Education Program

AIDS is an international disease. Today many countries have AIDS education programs to tell people about how AIDS is spread and how to protect themselves.

Work in a small group to plan an AIDS education program. Use the questions to help guide your discussion. Then present your plan to the class.

Planning the Program

Each student leads a discussion on one or two of the questions from the following worksheet. Each discussion leader should get ideas from the group and write down the final decisions that are made. (Remember to use the language for leading a discussion [see Section 6B].)

WORKSHEET

1. Who would the program be for (adults, young adults, high school age, elementary age, etc.)? _____

_____

2. What kind of program would it be? (Describe the program.) _____

_____

_____

_____

_____

3. Why would this kind of program be helpful? _____

_____

_____

_____

_____

4. What topics would be covered? _____

_____

_____

_____

_____

5. Where would the money for the program come from? _____

_____

6. What problems could there be with this program? How would you solve these problems?

_____

_____

_____

_____

_____

Presenting the Plan

After your discussion, prepare a group presentation of your plan to share with the class. Each group member reports on the question(s) that he/she led a discussion on.

Listening Task

As the leaders of each group present, think of one question to ask about their program. (Remember to use correct wh- question formation [see Section 6A].)

B. FIELDWORK

1. CALLING AN AIDS HOTLINE

a. Think of a question about AIDS. You can choose any topic, but make sure that your question is specific—for example, *What happens during an HIV blood test?* or *What is the latest treatment for AIDS?*

b. Look in your local telephone directory for the number of an AIDS hotline in your area. Call the hotline and ask your question.

c. Write the answer and share it with the class.

2. DOING A SURVEY

How much do people know about AIDS and HIV? Find three people outside your class to complete the quiz in Section 2A. How many questions did they get right? Share the results of the survey with the class.

ENGINE TROUBLE

1 APPROACHING THE TOPIC

A. PREDICTING

Look at the pictures of the cars. Read the title of the unit. Discuss these questions with a partner.

1. What does "Engine Trouble" mean?
2. What do you think this unit will be about?
3. What are the names of the cars? Write the names of the cars in the blanks.

   sports car   minivan   pick-up truck   sport utility vehicle (suv)

117

B. SHARING INFORMATION

1 *What is your favorite type of car? Why?*

2 *What do you look for when you buy a car? Look at the list. Add one idea of your own. Then rate the following things from most important **1** to least important **8**. Share your ideas with the class.*

_____ comfort	_____ style
_____ cost	_____ safety
_____ color	_____ size
_____ speed	_____ other: _____

2 PREPARING TO LISTEN

A. BACKGROUND

When you buy a car, there are many options you can choose, such as air conditioning, a radio, or four-wheel drive.

Read this report about four-wheel drive from a consumer magazine. Then look at the pictures on the next page of the car owners and their cars. Who should choose four-wheel drive as an option? Why? Share your ideas with a partner.

FOUR-WHEEL DRIVE OPTION

Description

Engine turns all four wheels instead of just two wheels. Greatly improves ability to drive in snow, ice, and mud. Not for use on dry, paved roads.

Recommendation

Easy to drive in snow, ice, and mud. Uses more gas and is expensive to repair.

B. VOCABULARY FOR COMPREHENSION

Read the conversations. Then circle the answer that best completes each definition.

1. A: Do you drive to work by yourself?

   B: No, I <u>carpool</u> with my co-workers.

   To <u>carpool</u> means to drive somewhere _____.

   a. alone
   b. with other people

2. A: Listen to the neighbors fighting! They must be really angry.

   B: Yeah. They are having a big <u>argument</u>.

   An <u>argument</u> is a _____.

   a. quiet discussion or conversation
   b. disagreement or fight

3. A: Do you live in the city or the country?

B: I live in between, in the <u>suburbs</u>.

The <u>suburbs</u> are _____.

a. far away from the city
b. just outside the city

4. A: What? We need to get gas again? We just got some yesterday.

B: I know. This car gets terrible <u>gas mileage</u>.

<u>Gas mileage</u> is the _____.

a. number of miles a car can go per gallon of gas
b. speed a car can go in a mile

5. A: I want to buy a sports car. Sports cars are <u>cool</u>!

B: Yeah. All your friends will want to go for a ride with you.

<u>Cool</u> means that something is _____.

a. stylish and fashionable
b. cold

6. A: There's something wrong with my car. It doesn't stop very well.

B: Oh, so your car doesn't <u>brake</u> very well.

To <u>brake</u> means to _____.

a. go faster
b. stop

7. A: The road to Jill's house is hard to drive on because of the holes and rocks.

B: That was five years ago. Now the road is <u>paved</u>, so driving is a lot easier.

A <u>paved</u> road is a _____ road.

a. smooth, modern
b. rough, dirt

8. A: Are you going to get a new car?

B: It <u>depends on</u> my old car. If my old car stops working, I'll have to buy a new one.

To <u>depend on</u> means that the result is _____.

a. certain
b. not yet certain

9. A: I heard there was a terrible car accident. A man drove into a tree.

   B: Yes. The driver was going very fast, and he couldn't <u>steer</u> the car.

   To <u>steer</u> means to _____.

   a. control the direction of a car
   b. drive a car backwards

10. A: We spend too much money on gas. We can't afford it.

    B: Well, then we have to <u>cut down on</u> the amount of gas we use.

    To <u>cut down on</u> means to _____.

    a. decrease
    b. increase

LISTENING ONE: Engine Trouble

A. INTRODUCING THE TOPIC

1 *You will hear a call-in radio program. The name of the show is* Engine Trouble. *People call the show for advice about cars and car repair. What do you think the show will be like? Circle one of the adjectives below.*

   serious   boring   funny

2 *Listen to the beginning of the radio show. Answer the questions.*

1. In your opinion, which word best describes Bob and Roy, the hosts of *Engine Trouble?* Circle one of the adjectives below.

   serious   boring   funny

   Why did you choose the word you did?

2. Do you think people can get helpful advice about car repair from this radio show? Why or why not?

B. LISTENING FOR MAIN IDEAS

Read the questions. Listen to the radio program. Circle the best answer.

1. Frank is calling *Engine Trouble* because he had an argument with
   _____.

   a. his friend
   b. Bob and Roy
   c. his wife

2. Frank _____ four-wheel drive when he drives to work.

   a. wants to use
   b. doesn't want to use
   c. doesn't know if he uses

3. Roy says that you shouldn't use four-wheel drive on roads that
   are _____.

   a. covered with ice
   b. covered with snow
   c. dry

4. Bob gives Frank advice about his car and _____.

   a. his marriage
   b. his job
   c. his house

5. At the end of the telephone call, Bob and Roy tell Frank
   _____.

   a. to buy a new car
   b. not to use four-wheel drive
   c. to get a divorce

C. LISTENING FOR DETAILS

 Listen to the radio program again. Who has these opinions? Check the appropriate column.

WHO HAS THESE OPINIONS?	FRANK	FRANK'S WIFE	BOB OR ROY	BOB'S WIFE
1. Doesn't like to carpool to work				
2. Thinks a four-wheel drive pickup truck is not a good car for the suburbs				
3. Thinks that having a pickup truck is cool				
4. Thinks that four-wheel drive will help the truck to brake better				
5. Says that four-wheel drive should not be used on dry roads				
6. Thinks that in marriage, it's more important to be happy than to be right				
7. Thinks that her husband is always wrong				
8. Thinks that Frank can stop using four-wheel drive and still make his wife happy				
9. Thinks that Frank's marriage can be happy if he tells his wife that she is right				
10. Jokes that Frank and his wife will get a divorce				

D. LISTENING BETWEEN THE LINES

People often use short words and sounds, such as *yes, right,* and *ah-hah,* to check comprehension or keep a conversation going.

Example

A: I went to Susan's house.

B: Huh? [*I didn't hear you.*]

A: I said, I went to Susan's house.

A: When I got to her house, I saw Russ's red sports car parked in her driveway.

B: Uh-huh. . . . [*I'm listening. Keep talking.*]

 Listen to excerpts from the radio show. Then draw lines to match the words or sounds with their meanings. Compare your answers with a partner.

Part 1

In excerpt 1, "Uh-huh" means . . .   **a.** "Yes."

In excerpt 2, "Huh?" means . . .   **b.** "I'm confused."

In excerpt 3, "Right!" means . . .   **c.** "I'm listening."

In excerpt 4, "Yeah" means . . .   **d.** "That's correct."

Part 2

In excerpt 5, "Ah-hah!" means . . .   **e.** "I didn't understand before, but now I do."

In excerpt 6, "See?" means . . .   **f.** "I just learned something important."

In excerpt 7, "Aaaahh" means . . .   **g.** "I'll do it."

In excerpt 8, "OK" means . . .   **h.** "Do you understand?"

4 LISTENING TWO: More Engine Trouble

A. EXPANDING THE TOPIC

Bob and Roy are still taking calls on *Engine Trouble*.

1. *Listen to the beginning of each call. Read the problems below and choose the best answer.*

2. *Work with a partner. Write a prediction about what you think Bob and Roy will tell each caller.*

3. *Now listen to the entire call. What advice did Bob and Roy give the caller? Take notes while you listen to the call. Write the advice.*

4. *With your partner, compare your predictions with your notes.*

PROBLEM	PREDICTION	ADVICE
Call 1 The caller wants to cut down on her _____ . **a.** driving **b.** gas mileage **c.** car insurance		
Call 2 The caller's husband won't _____ his old car. **a.** sell **b.** repair **c.** drive		
Call 3 The caller needs advice about _____ a car. **a.** repairing **b.** selling **c.** buying		

B. LINKING LISTENINGS ONE AND TWO

Discuss these questions with the class.

1. Do you think Bob and Roy give useful advice? Why or why not?

2. A radio show similar to *Engine Trouble* is very popular in the United States. Even people who don't own cars listen to it. Why do you think it is so popular? Would you listen to it?

3. Do you know of any other call-in radio shows? Do you listen to any of them? Which ones?

5 REVIEWING LANGUAGE

A. EXPLORING LANGUAGE: Intonation

In Section 3D, you heard some common words and sounds that people use to check comprehension or keep a conversation going. The meanings of the words and sounds may vary depending on how you say them. Saying a word with falling intonation usually expresses certainty: You are sure about what you are saying. We use falling intonation in statements. Saying a word with rising intonation usually expresses uncertainty: You are unsure of the answer. We use rising intonation in *yes/no* questions.

	Expression	Meaning
MECHANIC:	You're having trouble stopping in the rain, *right*?	Is that correct?
CAR OWNER:	*Right.*	That's correct.
MECHANIC:	First, I'll check the brakes, *OK*?	Is that all right?
CAR OWNER:	*OK.*	That's fine with me.

❶ Listen: *Listen to the conversation. Listen for the words* **right** *and* **OK** *and for the differences in their meanings.*

Read and Write: *Work with a partner. Read the conversation and decide which expression below goes in each blank. Write your answers in the blanks.*

Speak: *Practice the conversation with your partner. Make sure you use the correct intonation. Then switch roles and practice the conversation again.*

Right.	OK.
Right?	OK?

MECHANIC: What's the problem?

CAR OWNER: I was driving home last night and suddenly my car stopped for no reason.

MECHANIC: I see. But nothing unusual has happened before this, (1) _____

CAR OWNER: (2) _____ Everything has been normal.

MECHANIC: It might be a problem with your engine. I'm going to check that first, (3) _____

CAR OWNER: (4) _____ Do you know how long it will take for you to repair the car?

MECHANIC: Well, I can start working on it now. It will probably take a day to fix the problem.

CAR OWNER: So, you think it will be done tomorrow, (5) _____

MECHANIC: (6) _____ You can pick it up in the morning, (7) _____

CAR OWNER: (8) _____ But please call me if there are any problems.

2 *Listen again to the excerpts from Section 3D. Mark the intonation (with arrows) above the words and sounds to show whether the intonation rises or falls. The first one has been done for you. Compare your answers with a partner.*

Excerpt 1: Uh-huh.   Excerpt 5: Ah-hah!

Excerpt 2: Huh?   Excerpt 6: See?

Excerpt 3: Right!   Excerpt 7: Aaaahh.

Excerpt 4: Yeah.   Excerpt 8: OK.

B. WORKING WITH WORDS: Paraphrasing

1 *Write the vocabulary words from the unit after their definitions below.*

argument	cut down on	steer
dry	dummy	suburb
brake	practical	suddenly
carpool	gas mileage	terrible
cool	keep your mouth shut	vehicle

1. area just outside the city   _____

2. car or truck   _____

3. decrease   _____

4. direct or control direction   _____

5. don't say anything   _____

6. drive with others   _____

7. stylish and fashionable   _____

8. noisy disagreement   _____

9. quickly and unexpectedly   _____

10. stop   _____

11. a stupid person   _____

12. not wet   _____

13. sensible   _____

14. very bad   _____

15. amount of gas a car uses   _____

2 *Work with a partner. Student A will read a story one sentence at a time. After each sentence, Student B will check the information by replacing a word or phrase with a vocabulary word from Exercise 1.*

Example

A: I bought a small car because it doesn't use much gas.

B: Your car gets good *gas mileage*, right?

A: That's right.

Student A: Look at the exercise below.

Student B: See Student Activities, page 204.

Student A

1. *Read the sentences of the story to Student B one by one. Wait for Student B to check the information using a new vocabulary word. Tell your partner if the sentence is correct or not.*

   a. My coworker and I were driving home last night. We drive to and from work every day. (Answer: *carpool*)

   b. There was ice on the roads, but he didn't see the ice. (Answer: *dry*)

   c. He was driving too fast, and suddenly he couldn't control the car. (Answer: *steer*)

   d. He tried to stop the car. (Answer: *brake*)

   e. I told him not to make a quick stop on the ice. (Answer: *suddenly*)

   f. Then we had a fight. He told me not to tell him how to drive. (Answer: *argument*)

   g. I think next time I shouldn't say anything. (Answer: *keep your mouth shut*)

2. *Listen to Student B read a story. After each sentence, choose a vocabulary word to complete each sentence below. Read the sentence aloud. Your partner will tell you if you are correct.*

a. You didn't know what kind of _____ to get, right?

b. You wanted a car that looks _____, right?

c. Your friend says you made a _____ choice, right?

d. You live in the _____, right?

e. Four-wheel drive _____ gas mileage, right?

f. He thinks you need a more _____ car, right?

g. He thinks you're a _____, right?

6 GRAMMAR AND STYLE

A. GRAMMAR: Future Tense

1 *A reporter is interviewing a scientist about cars of the future. Read the interview. Notice the italicized words. They are future-tense verbs. Can you see how the future tense is used? Answer the questions below.*

REPORTER: What *will* cars *be* like in the future?

SCIENTIST: In the future, cars *are going to be* much better for the environment.

REPORTER: Why is that?

SCIENTIST: Well, one reason is that many cars *will run* on electricity instead of gas, so they *won't produce* as much pollution.

REPORTER: *Are* cars *going to look* the same?

SCIENTIST: In many ways, yes, but they will be much lighter, so they *aren't going to need* as much energy to run.

1. There are two ways to express the future tense. What are they? Which of these ways do you use more often?

2. What form do verbs take in the future tense? Find an example from the conversation that shows this form.

FOCUS ON GRAMMAR

See Future Tense in *Focus on Grammar, Intermediate.*

Future Tense	
a. Use *will* or *be going to* to make predictions about the future.	Cars **will (not)** be better in the future. Cars **are (not) going to** be cheaper.
b. Use *will* or *be going to* to ask questions about the future.	**Will** more people buy cars? What kind of cars **will** they buy? **Are** people **going to** drive less? Where **are** they **going to** drive?
c. In informal speech, we often use *contractions.*	Cars **won't** need as much energy. They**'ll** use less gas. Cars **aren't** going to be so large. They**'re** going to be smaller.
d. In informal speech, *going to* is pronounced *gonna.*	They're **gonna** be smaller.

2 *Work in pairs. Student A asks Student B questions about cars of the future. Use **will** and **be going to.** After Student B answers, Student A asks a follow-up question to get more information. Take turns asking and answering questions.*

Example: cars/be better for the environment

STUDENT A: In the future, will cars be better for the environment?

STUDENT B: Yes, they will.

STUDENT A: Why?

STUDENT B: Because they are going to use less gas.

1. cars/be smaller

2. people/drive less than they do now

3. cars/be more expensive

4. traffic/be worse

5. what type of car/be/the most popular

6. cars/run on gas or electricity

7. what new options/cars/have

8. what types of problem/cars/cause in the future

9. you/own a car in the future

10. [Ask your own question.] _____

B. STYLE: Checking Comprehension

If you don't understand what someone has said, you can check your comprehension by repeating the information you heard and asking the speaker if it is correct.

◆ **You think** cars will be smaller in the future, **right?**
◆ **You said that** cars will make less pollution, **right?**
◆ **You believe that** more people are going to buy cars, **right?**

If you understood correctly, the speaker will tell you that you are correct.

◆ **Right.**
◆ **That's right.**

If you didn't understand, the speaker will repeat the correct information.

◆ **No,** I think that cars will get bigger.

① *Read the sentences and complete them with one of the choices in parentheses. Write your complete sentence on a separate sheet of paper.*

1. Cars will be (bigger/smaller).

2. People are going to drive (less/more) than they do now.

3. Cars will be (less/more) expensive.

4. Traffic is going to be (better/worse).

5. (Minivans/sports cars) will be the most popular type of car.

6. Cars will run on (gas/electricity).

7. Cars (will/won't) be able to fly.

8. Cars are going to make (more/less) pollution in the future.

9. You (are/aren't) going to own a car in the future.

10. Trains will be (more/less) popular than cars.

2 *Work in pairs.*

Student A: Sit with your back to your partner and read your completed sentences as quickly as possible. When you are done, turn around and your partner will check his or her comprehension.

Student B: Sit with your back to your partner and listen to him or her say the sentences. As you listen, look at the sentences in your book and circle the words and phrases that your partner reads. Then turn around and check your answers. Use You think . . . right?; You said that . . . right?; *and* You believe that . . . right?

Then change roles.

7 ON YOUR OWN

A. SPEAKING TOPIC: Discussing the Future of Cars

Work in groups of four. Each member of the group chooses to read a different section of the following report on page 134, "The Future of the Automobile." Follow the steps below.

Step 1: Read only your section of the report. Do not read the other sections. Take notes using the chart on page 135. Take complete notes because you will be asked to share your summary with the other students in your group.

SPECIAL REPORT: *The Future of the Automobile*

Section 1: The Number of Cars

In 1995, there were 5 million cars in the world. Most of the cars were in the United States, Europe, and Japan. By 2030, there will be 1 billion cars in the world. The biggest increase in cars will probably be in Asia. For example, in 1995, there were 1.8 million cars in China, but by the year 2030, there will probably be 30 million. This big increase in cars will cause many new problems. Three of the major problems caused by cars will be with pollution, traffic, and the supply of oil.

Section 2: Future Problems

In the future, there will be many more cars in the world than there are today, so the problems caused by cars will only get worse. There are three main problems we need to solve. The first problem is air pollution from cars. Today more than 50 percent of the air pollution in cities is caused by cars, and the amount of pollution will increase when there are more cars. Second, the world's supply of oil will end in the next 100 years. As the oil supply decreases, gasoline will become more expensive. Then, when the oil supply ends, we won't be able to drive gasoline-powered cars at all. Finally, heavy traffic is already a terrible problem in many parts of the world. With more cars on the road, traffic will get worse.

Section 3: Possible Solutions I

We need to reduce air pollution and stop using a lot of oil and gasoline. To solve these problems, new types of cars are being developed. One type is the "supercar," which gets more than eighty miles per gallon. Some scientists believe that we can build a car that will get two hundred miles per gallon. These cars will use less gas, so they will make less pollution and save the oil supply. However, they will still need gasoline. Another type of car is the electric car. This car won't use oil at all. It will only use electricity. There are still some problems with electric cars. The batteries are expensive, and you must stop often to recharge the battery. However, these problems will probably be solved, and there will be new, better cars on the road.

Section 4: Possible Solutions II

There are some plans to reduce traffic problems in the future. One idea is to build "smart highways." These highways will have special computers that will be able to "talk" to the cars on the road. The computers will control the speed of cars on the highways, and help prevent accidents. Another plan is to build more public transportation. In the future, we will be able to build subways and trains that are faster and better than those we have today. However, people will need to change their habits: They will need to stop traveling by car and travel by public transportation instead.

Step 2: Work with your group. Each member presents his or her summary. After each presentation, check your comprehension. (Use the language in Section 6B.) Then use the chart to write notes for each section of the report.

SUMMARY

Section 1: The Number of Cars

Section 2: Future Problems

Section 3: Possible Solutions I

Section 4: Possible Solutions II

Step 3: Discuss these questions in your group or with the whole class.

a. Do most people in your country own cars, or only some people? Why? Do you think this will change in the future?

b. Does your country have problems with air pollution or traffic? How is your country trying to solve the problems?

c. Are there any other problems caused by cars in your country? How are they being solved?

d. What do you know about new types of cars that are being developed, including "supercars" and electric cars? Which type of new car will be the most useful?

e. What types of public transportation are used in your country? What new types do you think should be developed? Do you think your country should develop "smart highways"?

B. FIELDWORK

1. RESEARCH

Get information about new cars. Look in a newspaper or consumer magazine, or go to a car dealer. Find out about cost, gas mileage, and options such as four-wheel drive. Decide which car you like best, and why. Report back to the class.

2. INTERVIEW

Interview five people outside of your class. Write down their gender, age, and the number of people in their family. Then find out what their favorite type of car is and why. Use a form like this to write down the information:

Gender: Male   Female

Age: 16–25   26–40   41–65   65+

Number of people in your family: _____

Favorite type of car: _____

Reason: _____

_____

_____

Compare your information with other students in the class. What conclusions can you make about preferences for cars? Do men like different types of cars from women? Do people of different ages like different types of cars?

YOU ARE WHAT YOU WEAR

Shanika DeSilva from Sri Lanka

1 APPROACHING THE TOPIC

A. PREDICTING

Look at the photographs and discuss these questions with the class.

1. Where might the woman, Shanika DeSilva, wear her different outfits?

2. Are there any types of clothing that are not acceptable to wear in certain situations in your culture? If so, which outfits would not be acceptable? When and why would they not be acceptable?

3. The title of this unit is "You Are What You Wear." What does this mean? What do you think this unit will be about?

B. SHARING INFORMATION

Discuss these questions in a small group.

1. In your culture, what would you wear to go to the following places?

   ◆ An expensive restaurant

   ◆ A wedding

   ◆ Your home

   ◆ A grocery store

2. In the United States what would people wear in the places listed in Question 1? Are there any similarities or differences between what people wear in the United States and what people wear in your culture?

3. In your culture do women/men ever wear traditional clothing? What does it look like? When do they wear it?

PREPARING TO LISTEN

A. BACKGROUND

Read the paragraph. Then follow the directions.

There are many things which influence, or affect, our clothing style. We wear different clothes for different kinds of weather. We change our clothing depending on where we are: at home, at school, at work, and so on. We choose clothes that are acceptable for our sex, our age, our social class, or our religion. In some cultures, for instance, it might not be acceptable for older people to wear shorts or for women to show their hair. There are also customs about wearing traditional clothing. In some cultures people wear traditional clothing every day. In others it is only worn for weddings, holiday celebrations, and other special occasions. What we wear tells a lot about who we are and how we feel about the society in which we live.

*Look at the photographs of Shanika again. What can you tell about Shanika by the way she dresses? Read each statement and decide if it is true or false. Write **T or F**. In a small group, compare your opinions and discuss your reasons for your opinions.*

_____ 1. She has a job.

_____ 2. She likes to be fashionable.

_____ 3. She is proud of, or happy about, her culture.

_____ 4. She lives in the country (not the city).

_____ 5. She is poor.

_____ 6. She has had a lot of different experiences in her life.

_____ 7. She feels uncomfortable wearing Western clothing.

_____ 8. She wears traditional clothing more often than Western clothing.

_____ 9. She grew up in the United States.

_____ 10. She lives in the United States now.

B. VOCABULARY FOR COMPREHENSION

Read the sentences. Find the definition listed below that is closest in meaning to each underlined word. Write the letter in the blank.

a. affect

b. ways of feeling or thinking

c. took over the government of

d. events

e. it is not important

f. purpose

g. sensible

h. someone who works in government

i. from England

j. unusual

k. feeling of satisfaction or pleasure

l. usually

_____ 1. I <u>tend to</u> wear dresses in the summer. In fact, I hardly ever wear pants.

_____ 2. It isn't <u>practical</u> to wear traditional clothing for exercising because it's hard to move in.

_____ 3. He likes to wear traditional clothes for special <u>occasions</u> like holidays and religious celebrations.

_____ 4. Everyone is wearing jeans these days, so that's what I wear. I guess you can say that my friends <u>influence</u> what I wear.

_____ 5. Mr. Rajan, a <u>politician</u>, has been serving the Sri Lankan government for ten years.

_____ 6. England <u>colonized</u> Sri Lanka and ruled the country for over 100 years.

_____ 7. He was born in Britain, so he must be <u>British</u>.

_____ 8. He loves his culture so he wears traditional clothing to show his <u>pride</u>.

_____ 9. To me, <u>it doesn't matter</u> what I wear, but my mother feels that traditional clothing is an important part of my culture.

_____ 10. People's <u>attitudes</u> towards traditional clothing can change. Sometimes they want to wear it, and sometimes they don't.

_____ 11. When I was a child, I didn't understand the <u>value</u> of traditional clothes. I thought they were useless.

_____ 12. I like to wear my traditional clothing in the United States because people think it's <u>exotic</u>. Sometimes it's fun to wear something different from everybody else.

3 LISTENING ONE: Traditional Dress in Sri Lanka

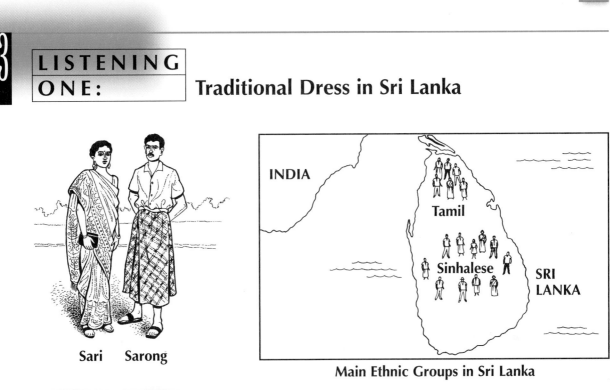

Sari   Sarong

Main Ethnic Groups in Sri Lanka

A. INTRODUCING THE TOPIC

You will hear an interview with Shanika De Silva about traditional clothes in Sri Lanka. Listen to this excerpt from the interview and answer the following questions.

1. Where is Shanika living?
2. Predict how Shanika feels about traditional dress.

B. LISTENING FOR MAIN IDEAS

Part 1

Below is a list of things that could influence people to wear or not wear traditional clothing. Read the list. Three of the topics are not mentioned in the listening exercise. Listen to Part 1 of the interview and check (✓) six topics that Shanika mentions. Compare your answers with a partner.

_____ **1.** age   _____ **4.** desire to be modern   _____ **7.** colonization

_____ **2.** comfort/discomfort   _____ **5.** cost   _____ **8.** opinion of friends

_____ **3.** pressure from family _____ **6.** family background   _____ **9.** political changes

Part 2

Listen to Part 2 of the interview. How does Shanika feel about traditional clothing? Circle the correct answers. Discuss your answers with the class.

1. She would _____ her daughter to wear traditional clothes.

   a. encourage   **b.** not encourage

2. When she was a child, she _____ to wear traditional clothes.

   a. liked   **b.** didn't like

3. As an adult she _____ to wear traditional clothes because they are different from what other people wear in the United States.

   a. likes   **b.** doesn't like

C. LISTENING FOR DETAILS

Listen again. Read each statement and decide if it is true or false. Write T or F. Compare your answers with a partner.

_____ 1. A sari goes around your waist and over one shoulder.

_____ 2. Younger women tend to wear saris.

_____ 3. Many younger women in Sri Lanka want to be modern.

_____ 4. Tamil women had relatives who wore Western clothing.

_____ 5. Today most men wear sarongs to work in an office.

_____ 6. When Sri Lanka was a British colony, the men wore Western clothes to work.

_____ 7. Politicians began wearing sarongs to work after the British left.

_____ 8. Shanika would like her son to have a sarong.

_____ 9. Shanika wore a sari for her wedding.

_____ 10. When she was younger, Shanika liked to wear jeans.

D. LISTENING BETWEEN THE LINES

1 *According to Shanika, people from Sri Lanka have both positive and negative feelings about traditional clothing. Listen to the following excerpts from the interview. For each excerpt, circle the number that you think best describes Shanika's feelings. The numbers are on a scale of 1–5, with 1 being positive and 5 being negative. As you listen, write down words and phrases that influence your answers.*

Excerpt	Positive				Negative
Excerpt 1	1	2	3	4	5
Excerpt 2	1	2	3	4	5
Excerpt 3	1	2	3	4	5
Excerpt 4	1	2	3	4	5
Excerpt 5	1	2	3	4	5

Words and Phrases That Influence Your Answers

Excerpt 1: _____

Excerpt 2: _____

Excerpt 3: _____

Excerpt 4: _____

Excerpt 5: _____

2 *Compare your answers with the class. Did you choose the same answers? Explain why you chose your answers.*

4 LISTENING TWO: Traditional Dress in Kuwait

A. EXPANDING THE TOPIC

Listen to another interview about traditional clothing. The speaker is Abdullah Al-Swaifan. He is from Kuwait. Circle the correct answers. Compare your answers with a partner.

1. What is a dishdasha?

   a. pants and a shirt
   b. a long shirt
   c. a big coat

2. What is a quitra and igal?

   a. socks and shoes
   b. pants and a shirt
   c. a type of hat

3. When do Kuwaiti men wear modern/Western clothing?

   a. for formal occasions
   b. for informal occasions
   c. for formal and informal occasions

4. What is an abaya?

   a. a black dress
   b. black pants and a shirt
   c. a big, black coat

5. What do most Kuwaiti women wear every day?

   a. an abaya
   b. dresses and jeans
   c. a long skirt

6. Does Abdullah wear traditional clothing when he is with his American friends? Why or why not?

B. LINKING LISTENINGS ONE AND TWO

1 Work in pairs. What are the similarities and differences between what people wear in Sri Lanka and what people wear in Kuwait? Check (✓) the type of clothing worn in different situations. Then compare the two cultures and check (✓) "similar" or "different." The first one is done for you.

SITUATION	CLOTHING IN SRI LANKA	CLOTHING IN KUWAIT	SIMILAR OR DIFFERENT?
1. A formal occasion (for example, a wedding)	**Men** ✓ Western ____ Traditional **Women** ____ Western ____ Traditional	**Men** ____ Western ✓ Traditional **Women** ____ Western ____ Traditional	**Men** ____ Similar ✓ Different **Women** ____ Similar ____ Different
2. An informal event (for example, a movie)	**Men** ____ Western ____ Traditional **Women** ____ Western ____ Traditional	**Men** ____ Western ____ Traditional **Women** ____ Western ____ Traditional	**Men** ____ Similar ____ Different **Women** ____ Similar ____ Different

2 *Discuss these questions in a small group.*

1. How do you feel about traditional clothing from your culture? Do you like to wear it? Why or why not? Do you feel more comfortable wearing it in your own culture than in another country? Why or why not?

2. Have you ever worn the clothing of another culture? If so, why did you wear it? How did it feel to wear it?

3. The title of this unit is "You Are What You Wear." Do you agree or disagree with this statement?

5 REVIEWING LANGUAGE

A. EXPLORING LANGUAGE: Thought Groups

Even though Shanika is from Sri Lanka, she sounds like a native English speaker. One of the reasons for her excellent pronunciation is that she pauses, or stops, between ideas. In English, it is important to pause between phrases that express complete ideas. This makes it easier for listeners to follow your thoughts.

Rule 1

If you are reading aloud, pause when you see a comma or a period.

Example

Written: Shanika De Silva, a native Sri Lankan, shares some comments on traditional dress.

Spoken: Shanika De Silva / a native Sri Lankan / shares some comments on traditional dress.

Rule 2

If you are speaking, pause briefly between ideas. There are no fixed rules for when ideas begin and end. Look for phrases that are normally grouped together—for example, nouns and articles, and prepositional phrases.

Example

Spoken incorrectly: People who live in the country still / wear saris.

Spoken correctly: People who live in the country / still wear saris.

1 **a.** *Read the following sentences from Listenings One and Two. Mark thought groups with slashes (/).*

1. Most of the older women, like my grandmother, wear a sari every day.

2. Saris are great for formal occasions, but if you're going out with your friends you want to be more modern.

3. Previous family history can influence the way you dress.

4. The men used to wear a sarong, which is a long piece of cloth that's wrapped around the waist.

5. People who have office jobs wear pants and shirts and even ties.

6. A dishdasha is like a long shirt with long sleeves.

7. For the summer we wear white ones and for the winter we have other colors.

8. On our heads we wear a quitra, which is a piece of cloth, and an igal, which is a piece of rope.

9. It's called an abaya, and it covers you completely.

10. If I wear it, I feel like everyone's looking at me.

b. *Now work with a partner. Student A reads sentences 1–5. Student B reads 6–10. Listen to your partner and agree or disagree with the way he or she reads each sentence.*

c. *Listen to all ten sentences on the tape. Check your markings. There may be some small differences between your markings and the pauses you hear. Some of the differences may be fine. Some may be incorrect. Discuss any questions with the class.*

❷ *Sometimes if you pause in the wrong place you can change the meaning of a sentence. Match each sentence with its meaning. The first one is done for you.*

Work in pairs. Student A reads either (a) or (b) for each number 1–4, and Student B listens and chooses the correct meaning (c) or (d). Then, Student B reads either (a) or (b) for each number 5–8, and Student A chooses the correct meaning (c) or (d).

1. **a.** She wore a pretty old dress.

   b. She wore a pretty, / old dress.

   c. The dress was pretty and old.

   d. The dress was very old.

2. **a.** He's wearing a light blue sweater.

   b. He's wearing a light, / blue sweater.

   c. The sweater isn't heavy.

   d. The color of the sweater is light blue.

3. **a.** We had fruit, / cake, / and coffee / after the fashion show.

   b. We had fruitcake and coffee / after the fashion show

   c. There were two things to eat.

   d. There was one thing to eat.

4. **a.** The fashion magazine had two photos / of a woman and a man.

   b. The fashion magazine / had two photos / of a woman / and a man.

   c. There was one person in each photo.

   d. There were two people in each of the photos.

5. **a.** We're buying the dress for Sally, / Paul.

   b. We're buying the dress for Sally Paul.

   c. Sally's last name is Paul.

   d. The speaker is talking to Paul.

6. **a.** "Sally," / said Paul, /"hates dresses."

   b. Sally said, / "Paul hates dresses."

   c. Paul hates dresses.

   d. Sally hates dresses.

7. **a.** I bought red shoes and socks.

   b. I bought red shoes / and socks.

   c. The socks are red.

   d. We don't know the color of the socks.

8. **a.** We bought her a hat / pin / and scarf.

   b. We bought her a hat pin / and scarf.

   c. We gave her two presents.

   d. We gave her three presents.

B. WORKING WITH WORDS: Analogies

An **analogy** shows relationships between words. Below are four types of analogies that show different kinds of relationships. Read an analogy this way: "Fly is to plane as drive is to car."

Analogies

Action/Object fly : plane :: drive : car	Shows what action is used with an object. You **fly** a **plane**. You **drive** a **car**.
Opposite love : hate :: fast : slow	Shows two opposite things. The opposite of **love** is **hate**. The opposite of **fast** is **slow**.
Description water : wet :: ice : cold	Shows what something is by describing it. **Water** is **wet**. **Ice** is **cold**.
Part/Whole student : class :: eye : body	Shows a small part of something larger. A **student** is part of a **class**. An **eye** is part of the **body**.

1 *Work with a partner. Choose the correct word from the list below to complete each analogy. For each analogy write two explanation sentences like the example sentences in the chart on page 149.*

Sri Lanka	modern	old-fashioned
sari	political	Britain
colonize	exotic	independent

1. London : Britain :: Colombo : _____

Explanation sentences: _____

_____

2. practical : impractical :: modern : _____

Explanation sentences: _____

_____

3. put on : pants :: wrap : _____

Explanation sentences: _____

_____

4. sari : traditional :: jeans : _____

Explanation sentences: _____

_____

5. young : old :: dependent : _____

Explanation sentences: _____

_____

6. Sri Lankan : Sri Lanka :: British : _____

Explanation sentences: _____

_____

2 *Read the beginnings of the four analogies. Complete the analogies using your own words.*

   a. formal : informal :: _____ : _____

   b. Levi's : jeans :: _____ : _____

   c. wear : sarong :: _____ : _____

   d. dishdasha : men :: _____ : _____

Walk around the class. Tell your analogies to people in your class, but only give them the first three words. Ask them to guess the last word. Give them three chances to guess each analogy before you give the answer.

Example

   STUDENT A: Formal, informal. Weak, . . .
   STUDENT B: Strong.

6 SKILLS FOR EXPRESSION

A. GRAMMAR: *Used To*

1 *In the interview, Shanika talks about what men **used to** wear in Sri Lanka. Underline the phrases with **used to** and the verbs that follow. The first one has been done for you. Then answer the questions below.*

The men in Sri Lanka <u>didn't use to wear</u> pants. Instead, they used to have special cloths around their waists called sarongs. When the British arrived, the men changed to Western clothing; but after the British left, many politicians who used to wear suits to work started to wear sarongs again.

   1. Look at the phrases you underlined. Why does the speaker use *used to* instead of the simple past tense?

   2. In the last sentence the speaker uses the simple past instead of *used to*. Why?

FOCUS ON GRAMMAR

See Used to in *Focus on Grammar, Intermediate.*

Used to

Use **used to** to talk about repeated actions, states, or habits in the past that usually don't happen anymore.

a. To make a statement with **used to** ◆ Use **used to** + base form of verb.	The politicians **used to wear** suits, but now they wear sarongs.
b. To make a negative with **used to** ◆ Use **didn't** ◆ Remove **d** from **used**.	The men **didn't use to wear** pants, but now they do.

2 *Work in pairs. Look at these pictures of Shanika's mother as a young woman in Sri Lanka and as an older woman in the United States. Student A begins a sentence by telling what Shanika's mother used to wear for formal occasions. Student B completes the sentence by telling what Shanika's mother wears now. Take turns beginning and completing the sentences.*

Example

STUDENT A: Shanika's mother used to wear dark-colored lipstick . . .

STUDENT B: . . . but now she wears light-colored lipstick.

B. STYLE: Oral Presentation Introductions

When you give a speech, or oral presentation, it is important to introduce the topic of the presentation before you begin talking about it. This helps to prepare the audience to listen.

1 *Read the phrases (things to say) and the techniques (things to do) that can be used to introduce a speech.*

Introducing a Speech

Phrases

* Today I'd like to talk about _____.

* My topic for today is _____.

* _____ is the topic of my presentation today.

Techniques

* Begin with one of the phrases above.

* Begin with a question. Then use one of the phrases above.

    What do you wear when you go to work?

* Begin with a statement about the topic. Then use one of the phrases above.

    Jeans have become a kind of uniform for people all over the world . . .

Note: When you state your topic, make sure that you are specific.

    Today I'd like to talk about **jeans.** (too general)

    Today I'd like to talk about **how jeans have influenced the way people dress at work.** (specific)

2 *Read the list of general oral presentation topics. Choose three topics and make them more specific. Then prepare an introduction for each topic. Use the outline on page 154 to help you plan each introduction.*

Oral Presentation Topics

uniforms	traditional clothing	body piercing
gang clothing	teenage fashions	brand-name clothes
clothing for the office	men's vs. women's clothing	hairstyles

General topic: _____

Specific topic: _____

First sentence: _____

_____.

Notes on other things you would like to say:

◆ _____

◆ _____

◆ _____

Meet in a small group. Take turns presenting your introductions. After each introduction the other students in the group will predict what topics they think the rest of the presentation will include.

ON YOUR OWN

A. SPEAKING TOPIC: Impromptu Speeches

Impromptu speeches are speeches that you make without much preparation. Making an impromptu speech will challenge you to think quickly and will also give you practice talking in front of a group.

Topic

Some fashions come and go. People wear them for a short time and then don't wear them again. Other fashions continue for a long time, and some may even change the way people dress forever. Here is a list of fashions that have influenced the way people dress today.

Fashions That Have Influenced History

bikinis	high heels	athletic shoes	pants for women
shorts	miniskirts	nail polish	dying hair
jeans	T-shirts	baggy (gang) pants	perming hair

Work in a group of six or seven.

a. Write each of the fashions from the list on page 154 on a separate piece of paper and put the papers in a bag.

b. Student A picks a piece of paper from the bag and leaves the classroom for five minutes to prepare a speech on the topic he/she picked. Student A returns.

c. Before Student A presents, Student B picks a piece of paper and goes outside to prepare.

d. While Student B is preparing, Student A gives his/her speech to the rest of the group (three minutes) and then discusses the topic with the group (two minutes).

e. Student B returns. Before Student B presents, Student C picks a piece of paper and goes outside to prepare.

f. Continue until everyone has given a presentation.

When you prepare your speech, don't write it out. You won't have time. Just make brief notes.

Outline for Presentation

Here is an outline for you to follow as you present.

a. Describe the fashion item.

b. What did people use to do/wear in your culture before this fashion was invented? (Remember to use the correct grammar for *used to* [see Section 6A].)

c. What do people in your culture do/wear now as a result of this fashion?

d. Do you like this fashion? Why or why not?

When you present, remember to introduce your topic (see Section 6B) and pause between thought groups (see Section 5A).

Listening Task

As you listen to each presentation, think of these questions:

a. How do people in your culture feel about this fashion item?

b. Compare the view of this fashion item in your culture with that in the speaker's culture.

Be prepared to share your thoughts during the discussion time after the presentation.

B. FIELDWORK

1. MAGAZINE PICTURES

Bring in a magazine picture of someone who dresses distinctively—for example, a teenager, a movie star, a farmer, or a politician. Show the picture to the class and talk about what that person's clothes tell us about him/her—for example, the job the person does, whether he/she has a lot of money, his/her personality, and so on.

Listening Task

Listen to the other students' presentations. Do you agree or disagree with their interpretations? Be prepared to give your opinion.

2. PRESENTATION FOR THE CLASS

Bring in an item of traditional clothing from your home culture and show it to the class. (If you don't have any traditional clothing, bring a picture.) Talk about the following:

a. the name of the clothing

b. who wears it

c. when it is worn

d. whether or not you wear it

e. any other interesting information

Listening Task

As each student presents, think of one question that you can ask him/her about his/her traditional clothing.

TO SPANK OR NOT TO SPANK?

1 APPROACHING THE TOPIC

A. PREDICTING

Look at the picture. Read the title of the unit. Discuss these questions with the class.

1. Why do you think the parent is spanking the child? What did he do?
2. Do you think spanking is a good punishment here?
3. What do you think the unit will be about?

B. SHARING INFORMATION

Discuss these questions in a small group.

1. How did your parents punish you? How did you feel about the punishment then? How do you feel about it now?

2. Do you think it is a good idea for parents to punish their children by spanking or hitting them? Why or why not? What other types of punishment could parents use?

PREPARING TO LISTEN

A. BACKGROUND

Read the paragraph. Then follow the directions.

Ideas about how to punish children have changed over time. Also, they differ from culture to culture and family to family. Some parents believe that spanking children is the best way to punish. Others think that parents should never hit their children. Most parents punish their children in the same way that they were punished by their parents. Although all parents agree that children must learn the difference between right and wrong, there is a lot of disagreement about the best way to teach them this lesson.

❶ *A ten-year-old boy did something wrong. How should his parents punish him? Read the four situations at the top of the chart on page 159. Then read the possible things the boy's parents could do to punish him. Put a check (✓) next to the punishments you think are best in each situation. (You can check more than one possible punishment.)*

❷ *Compare your answers with those of the other students and explain your choices.*

HOW SHOULD PARENTS PUNISH A TEN-YEAR-OLD BOY WHO . . .	BROKE A WINDOW WHILE PLAYING BALL IN THE HOUSE?	HIT ANOTHER CHILD?	STOLE MONEY FROM A PARENT?	STARTED A FIRE WHILE PLAYING WITH MATCHES?
1. Yell at the child				
2. Send the child to bed without dinner				
3. Not let the child watch TV for a week				
4. Make the child do an unpleasant task, such as clean the bathroom				
5. Spank the child				
6. Hit the child with a belt or stick				
7. [other] _____ _____				

B. VOCABULARY FOR COMPREHENSION

The following letter was written to a newspaper advice column. Read the letter. Then match the boldfaced words and phrases with the definitions below. Write the numbers in the blanks.

City Herald   Monday, September 8

Dear Gabby
Gabigail Van Danders

Dear Gabby,

My husband and I disagree about how to **discipline** our children. We have different ideas about how to punish them when they **misbehave,** or do something bad. He thinks that it's **acceptable** to spank them, but I think it is not right to hit them. He says that we should do it **for their own good,** so our children will learn right and wrong. He says our children must **respect** us, so they will listen to us and do what we say.

I disagree. I believe that spanking, hitting, or any **corporal punishment** is a form of **child abuse** and is very harmful to children. I think it is a form of **violence.** It's easy to **go too far** and hurt them by mistake, even leaving a **bruise** or other mark on their body. I think people who hit children should **be arrested** by the police and put in jail. To tell the truth, I **admit** that I sometimes feel like hitting my children when I am very angry, but I think it's wrong. What should my husband and I do?

Signed, Confused Mom

_____ **a.** actions that cause hurt or harm

_____ **b.** obey

_____ **c.** all right

_____ **d.** go beyond the limit

_____ **e.** treatment that hurts a child

_____ **f.** do something wrong

_____ **g.** in order to help them

__1__ **h.** punish

_____ **i.** a dark mark on the body caused by being hit

_____ **j.** tell the truth

_____ **k.** punishment that physically hurts the body

_____ **l.** be taken by the police for committing a crime

3 LISTENING ONE: A Radio Report

Dale Clover, arrested for spanking his son

A. INTRODUCING THE TOPIC

Listen to an excerpt of the report. Answer the questions.

1. What opinion do you think will be presented in the report?

   _____ Supporting spanking

   _____ Opposing spanking

   _____ Both opinions

   What words did you hear that made you choose your answer?

2. The reporter interviews several different people in this report. Who do you think will give an opinion about spanking?

   _____ Police officer   _____ Parent   _____ Teacher

   _____ Doctor   _____ Child

B. LISTENING FOR MAIN IDEAS

 In the report you will hear different people's opinions about spanking. You will also hear many reasons for their opinions. Do the people being interviewed support spanking (think it's good) or oppose spanking (think it's bad)? Listen to the report and check (✓) each person's opinion. Then write at least one reason for each opinion.

SPEAKER	OPINION		REASON(S)
	Support	**Oppose**	
1. Dale Clover			
2. Rhonda Moore			
3. Taylor Robinson			
4. Dr. John Oparah			
5. Dr. Beverly Lau			

C. LISTENING FOR DETAILS

*You have listened to the speakers' opinions and have identified at least one reason for each opinion. Now listen for all of the reasons. What does each speaker believe about spanking? Write Y for "yes" if the statement expresses the speaker's beliefs. Write N for "no" if the statement does **not** express the speaker's beliefs.*

Dale Clover, parent

_____ **1.** Spanking is the only way to keep my son out of trouble.

Rhonda Moore, parent

_____ **2.** Pain helps children learn right and wrong.

_____ **3.** Spanking is done out of anger.

_____ **4.** Her children don't understand why they are spanked.

Taylor Robinson, parent

_____ **5.** Spanking teaches children to solve problems with violence.

_____ **6.** Spanking teaches children to talk about problems.

Dr. John Oparah, doctor

_____ **7.** Many children don't respect their parents.

_____ **8.** Parents who spank should be treated like criminals.

_____ **9.** Some children say they will call the police if their parents spank them.

Dr. Beverly Lau, doctor

_____ **10.** Children who are spanked misbehave less often.

_____ **11.** Children who are spanked are less violent.

_____ **12.** Eighty-five percent of cases of serious child abuse start when a parent spanks a child and the punishment goes too far.

D. LISTENING BETWEEN THE LINES

Parents often say to their children, "Do as I say, not as I do." For example, parents who smoke cigarettes may tell their children, "Don't smoke." Children learn, however, not only by listening to what their parents say, but by watching what their parents do. We don't always know which has a stronger effect.

1 *What do parents and doctors believe about how children learn? Do they think that children learn more by watching what their parents do or by listening to what their parents say? Listen to the excerpts from the radio report. Each speaker has an opinion about how children learn. Check (✓) each speaker's opinion in the chart. Then write the reasons for the opinions. Compare your answers with your classmates.*

| SPEAKER | CHILDREN LEARN BY | | REASON |
	WATCHING	LISTENING	
Excerpt 1 Rhonda Moore			
Excerpt 2 Tayler Robinson			
Excerpt 3 Dr. John Oparah			
Excerpt 4 Dr. Beverly Lau			

2 *Discuss the following question with the class.*

How do you think children learn: by watching what parents do or by listening to what parents say? Why?

4 LISTENING TWO: Expert Opinions

A. EXPANDING THE TOPIC

What are the effects of spanking as children get older and become adults? Listen to four people's opinions about the long-term effects of spanking. Listen once and check (✓) if each person supports or opposes spanking. Then listen again and write the reason for his or her opinion.

Fill in the chart with the information you hear.

SPEAKER	OPINION		REASON(S)
	Support	Oppose	
1. Donald Sterling			
2. Dr. Phyllis Jones			
3. Dr. Armando Mazzone			
4. Lois Goldin			

B. LINKING LISTENINGS ONE AND TWO

① *Read the list of opinions supporting spanking and opposing spanking. Which ones do you agree with? Which ones do you disagree with? Discuss your answers in a small group. Give reasons for your own opinions.*

Opinions Supporting Spanking

Pain helps children learn.

Spanking teaches children to respect their parents.

Spanking stops children from becoming criminals.

Opinions Opposing Spanking

Spanking teaches children to be violent.

Spanking can seriously hurt children.

Spanking is not an effective punishment.

② *Discuss these questions in a small group.*

1. Compare beliefs about spanking and discipline in the United States with beliefs in other cultures. Use information you heard in the listenings. How are the beliefs similar? How are they different?

2. Corporal punishment is sometimes used to punish students in school, criminals in jail, and soldiers in the military. Do you support corporal punishment in these situations? Do you support corporal punishment in any other situations? Why or why not?

3. Do you think parents discipline their sons differently from their daughters? If so, what are these differences? Why do you think there are differences?

5 REVIEWING LANGUAGE

A. EXPLORING LANGUAGE: Prefixes

A **prefix** is a short word or syllable that can be added to the beginning of some words. A prefix can change the meaning of a word. The following prefixes all express the meaning *not* or *opposite*.

Prefix	Meaning	Example	Meaning
dis-	not	**disagree**	not agree
mis-	not; badly or not correctly	**misbehave**	behave badly
non-	opposite of; without	**nonviolence**	without violence
un-	not	**unacceptable**	not acceptable

❶ *Read the sentences below and on page 168. Add the correct prefix to the words. Use a dictionary to help you.*

1. That child's behavior is not acceptable. It is _____ acceptable.

2. He never obeys his parents. He always _____ obeys their rules.

3. He doesn't use his family's money wisely. He _____ uses it.

4. I feed my family foods without fat. I give them _____ fat foods.

5. I don't approve of spanking. I _____ approve of it.

6. Some children are just not friendly. They are _____ friendly.

7. I spank my son when he doesn't behave. When he _____ behaves, spanking helps.

8. My sister thinks spanking is not kind. She says it's _____ kind.

9. I don't like to punish my child. I _____ like punishing her.

10. She never pronounces her grandchildren's names correctly. She _____ pronounces their names.

11. Children should be punished if they are not respectful. Punishment can stop kids from being _____ respectful.

12. My daughter never stops talking. She talks _____ stop.

13. My sister doesn't understand why I spank my children. She _____ understands my reasons for spanking.

14. The kind of punishment you use is not important. It's _____ important.

15. His parents only have drinks with no alcohol at home. They only have _____ alcoholic drinks.

2 *Work in pairs. Student A reads below. Student B turn to page 205.*

Student A, Part 1

Student A: Read sentences 1–10 to Student B. Your partner will repeat the sentences, changing the underlined words to a word with a prefix. Tell your partner if his/her answer is correct. (The correct answers are in parentheses.)

1. Children <u>don't like</u> getting punished. (dislike)

2. Doctors recommend punishment that is <u>not violent</u>. (nonviolent)

3. Hitting a child is <u>not</u> an <u>acceptable</u> type of punishment. (unacceptable)

4. What did she say? I <u>didn't understand correctly</u>. (misunderstood)

5. The boy <u>doesn't obey</u> his teacher. (disobeys)

6. Good grades in school are <u>not important</u> to my daughter. (unimportant)

7. The children <u>behaved badly</u> today. (misbehaved)

8. This airplane flies <u>without stops</u> to Hawaii. (nonstop)

9. Some children are <u>not respectful</u> to their parents. (disrespectful)

10. I think spanking is <u>not kind</u>. (unkind)

Part 2

Listen to Student B read sentences 11–20. Read the sentences below back to your partner, filling in the space with a word with a prefix. Your sentence should have the same meaning as the sentence Student B reads to you. Your partner will tell you if your answer is correct.

11. Violent behavior is _____.

12. He is _____.

13. I always _____ that word.

14. I like beer that is _____.

15. _____ ice cream is healthier.

16. Many parents _____ of spanking.

17. I _____ punishing my children.

18. Parents _____ about spanking.

19. She _____ her computer, so it broke.

20. We teach children that hitting other people is

    _____.

B. WORKING WITH WORDS: Stronger vs. Weaker Language

Look at the example. One of the words does not make sense in the sentence.

Parents who support spanking feel that spanking is _____ .
acceptable ~~terrible~~ (good)

Use a dictionary to look up any words you don't know. Cross out the one word that doesn't belong. Then decide which of the two remaining words has a stronger meaning. Circle the stronger word. Discuss your answers in a small group.

1. Did your parents _____ you when you did something wrong?
   beat   spank   reward

2. It is wrong for parents to _____ their children.
   be unkind to   abuse   take care of

3. Strong discipline teaches children to _____ their parents.
   remember   like   respect

4. Many doctors feel that spanking is too _____ .
   violent   gentle   rough

5. Some parents spank their children when they _____ .
   misbehave   are good   make a mistake

6. Children who are abused can become _____ adults.
   aggressive   quiet   abusive

7. Back problems in adults may be a _____ effect of spanking children.
   serious   terrible   positive

8. Parents often abuse their children when they are _____ .
   angry   annoyed   calm

9. Parents will continue to _____ how to discipline their children.

agree about   talk about   debate

10. Parents who don't spank their children _____ spanking as a form of punishment.

disagree with   support   oppose

6 SKILLS FOR EXPRESSION

A. GRAMMAR: Present Perfect

❶ *Read the paragraph. Notice the verbs in the present perfect tense. Then answer the questions below.*

The number of parents who spank their children in the United States *has decreased* in the past fifty years. Public opinion about spanking *has changed*. Many doctors *have said* that spanking is harmful—or is even a form of child abuse. Parents *have learned* new ways to discipline their children. However, at the same time, the number of crimes committed by children *hasn't gone down*, it *has increased*.

1. How is the present perfect tense formed?

2. When do we use the present perfect tense?

3. When do we use the simple past tense?

FOCUS ON GRAMMAR

See Present Perfect Tense in *Focus on Grammar, Intermediate.*

Present Perfect Tense

a. Use the present perfect ◆ To talk about things that happened at an unspecific time in the past ◆ To talk about things that started in the past, continue up to the present, and may continue into the future	Many doctors **have said** that spanking is harmful. (We don't know when they said this.) The number of parents who spank their children in the United States **has decreased** in the past 100 years. (The number started decreasing in the past and will probably continue to decrease.)
b. To form the present perfect * ◆ Use **have/has** + the past participle	Public opinion about spanking **has changed.** People **have learned** new ways to discipline their children.
c. To form a negative ◆ Add **not** after **have/has**	The number of crimes **has not gone** down.
d. To form questions ◆ **Yes/no** questions begin with **have/has** ◆ **Wh-** questions begin with a **wh-** word Note: **Have/has** are usually contracted in informal speech.	**Have** you **read** the report about spanking? Why **have** you **stopped** spanking your child? He**'s stopped** spanking his child.

*The regular form of the past participle is sometimes the simple past form of the verb. For a list of irregular past participles, see *Focus on Grammar, Intermediate,* Appendix .

2 *In the United States, beliefs about spanking and discipline have changed over time. How have beliefs changed in other cultures? Complete these statements with the present perfect. Compare your answers in a small group.*

Changes in beliefs about spanking and corporal punishment in the past fifty years:

1. Parents' beliefs about spanking ___have changed___ (change) in the United States. Many parents _____ (stop) using spanking as their most important method of discipline.

2. The United States government _____ (pass) stronger laws against child abuse. Police _____ (arrest) more parents for abusing their children.

3. Many American doctors _____ (advise) parents not to spank their children. They _____ (suggest) using nonviolent methods of discipline.

4. The number of crimes committed by children and teenagers _____ (rise) in the United States. Some people believe this is because parents _____ (not/teach) their children right and wrong.

5. American teachers _____ (stop) using corporal punishment in the classroom. The government _____ (decide) that it is against the law for teachers to hit their students.

3 *Stay in your groups. Take turns asking and answering the following questions. First complete the questions with the present perfect. Then give answers about a culture with which you are familiar.*

1. How _____ parents' beliefs about discipline _____ (change)?

2. What kind of laws against child abuse _____ the government _____ (pass)?

3. How _____ doctors _____ (advise) parents to discipline their children?

4. _____ the number of crimes committed by children _____ (rise) or _____ (fall)?

5. How _____ discipline in schools _____ (change)?

B. STYLE: Supporting Your Opinions

❶ *If you want to persuade someone to agree with you, it is necessary to support, or explain, your opinions. Look at the four common ways to support your opinions.*

Ways to Support Your Opinions

Facts Give facts to show that your ideas are based on true information, not just on feelings.	Spanking helps to prevent crime, not increase it. The reason for my opinion is the fact that crime has increased as spanking has decreased. In the 1950s, for example, spanking was a more common form of punishment than it is today. And in the 1950s, the crime rate was lower than it is today.
Statistics Give numbers to show that your ideas are based on research.	I strongly oppose spanking because it can turn into child abuse. I say this because 85 percent of child abuse cases start when the parent disciplines the child using corporal punishment.
Examples Describe a situation to explain what you are talking about.	I don't think that spanking teaches children anything. Let me give you an example. What if a child hits his friend, and is then spanked as punishment? He may be very confused about when hitting is bad, and when it's OK.
Personal stories Tell a personal story to show that your ideas are based on experience.	I think spanking helps children learn. For instance, I once stole some candy from the store. My father spanked me when he found out. I always remembered that spanking, and I never stole anything again.

There are many phrases that you can use to introduce support. Some are listed below.

Introducing Support

- For example . . .
- For instance . . .
- Let me give you an example.

- I say this because . . .
- The reason for my opinion is . . .

---

2 *Discuss the four types of support. Which do you think are more persuasive? Which are less persuasive? For example, are facts more persuasive than personal stories? Why or why not? Explain your answers.*

3 *Read the two discussion topics below. First decide if you agree or disagree with each statement. Then write down a fact, statistic, personal story, or example to support your opinion. Work in a small group. Discuss each topic for five minutes. Use the notes you wrote to help support your opinions.*

Discussion Topic 1

Parents should spank their children.

Opinion: Agree/Disagree

Support: _____

_____

_____

Discussion Topic 2

Teachers should be allowed to spank their students.

Opinion: Agree/Disagree

Support: _____

_____

_____

Report to the class. What types of support did your classmates give? Which support was the most persuasive? Why?

7 ON YOUR OWN

A. SPEAKING TOPIC: Debate

1. CHOOSE A TOPIC

a. Divide into two teams. One team will be the **For** team (the team that supports the topic) and the other team will be the **Against** team (the team that opposes the topic).

b. Choose one of the debate topics below. (If you have a large class, you may divide into groups and have several debates on different topics.)

Debate Topics

Topic 1: *It should be against the law for parents to spank their children.*

Some countries have passed laws that say it is wrong for parents to hit or spank their children. In other countries, parents can punish their children however they want.

Topic 2: *Teachers should spank their students as a form of discipline in school.*

In some countries, teachers can hit or spank their students when the students misbehave. In other schools, it is against the law for teachers to hit their students.

Topic 3: *Governments should use corporal punishment as a way to punish criminals.*

In some countries, the government uses corporal punishment (hitting or beating) to punish criminals. In other countries, the government can't use corporal punishment.

Topic 4: *Parents should be punished when their children do something wrong.*

In the United States, some people want to pass a new law that says if a child under eighteen does something wrong (such as stealing from a store or missing school), the parents will be punished because they did not control their child.

2. PLAN THE DEBATE

Each team will work together to plan the debate. You will plan what to say in support of your opinion and how to argue against the other team. There are three steps to planning the debate.

Step 1: Explain and Defend Your Team's Ideas

a. Think of three main points, or arguments, to support your opinion. Support your points, facts, statistics, examples, and personal stories (see Section 6B.)

b. Think of arguments the other team might make against your main points. Decide what to say to defend your ideas or to show that your ideas are correct.

c. Use an outline like this to help you plan:

Main Points That Support Your Team's Opinion

Main point: _____

Support: _____

_____

Possible argument against point: _____

_____

What you will say to defend point: _____

_____

Step 2: Prepare to Speak against the Other Team

a. Think of three possible main points that you think the other team will make to support their opinion.

b. Decide what you will say to show that the other team is wrong. When expressing opposition make sure you use prefixes of opposition (see Section 5A).

c. Use an outline like this to help you plan:

Main Points to Support the Other Team's Opinion

Other team's main point: _____

Explanations and examples that show they are wrong: _____

_____

Step 3: Divide the Speaking Tasks

Each team member will talk during the debate. Decide which team member will explain each part of the debate.

3. HAVE THE DEBATE

Follow the structure below.

a. *For* team explains its first point.

b. *Against* team members discuss briefly among themselves, and then argue against *For* team's point.

c. *Against* team explains its first point.

d. *For* team members discuss briefly among themselves, and then argue against *Against* team's point.

e. The debate continues in this way until both teams make their main points.

B. FIELDWORK

OBSERVATION

Visit a place where you can see adults taking care of young children. For example, visit a nursery or preschool, go to a playground, or visit a friend or relative who has children. Watch the children and adults for an hour or so. Look for times when a child misbehaves and an adult disciplines the child. Use the chart to take notes about what you see. Answer these questions:

WHY DID THE ADULTS DISCIPLINE THE CHILDREN?	HOW DID THE ADULTS DISCIPLINE THE CHILDREN?	WAS IT EFFECTIVE?
A child threw something at another child	An adult yelled and said not to throw things.	No

Here are some things an adult may do to discipline a child (but look for other things that are not on this list):

Say "No" to the child
Take something away from the child
Move the child to a different place
Make the child sit by himself or herself
Hold the child so he or she can't do something
Yell at the child in a loud voice
Hit or spank the child

Make a tape recording of your observations. Answer these questions about what you saw. When you are finished, give the tape to your teacher.

a. What types of discipline did you see? Was the discipline violent or nonviolent?

b. Did the discipline make the child stop misbehaving? Why or why not?

c. What does this type of discipline teach a child?

d. How was the discipline the same or different from other types of discipline you have seen or experienced?

Discuss your observations with the class.

A MARRIAGE AGREEMENT

HE WON'T WEAR A SUIT. HE SAYS IT ISN'T IN OUR MARRIAGE AGREEMENT.

1 APPROACHING THE TOPIC

A. PREDICTING

Look at the cartoon. Discuss these questions with the class.

1. Where are the man and woman?

2. Why is the husband dressed differently from everyone else?

3. How does the wife feel? Why does she feel this way?

4. In a marriage agreement, two people write down rules for how they will live together. Who do you think would write a marriage agreement? What would be included?

B. SHARING INFORMATION

Discuss these questions in a small group.

1. What makes a marriage happy or unhappy? Below are two lists of reasons, one for happy marriages and one for unhappy marriages. Add three ideas to each list.

A Happy Marriage	An Unhappy Marriage
a. trust	**a.** difficulty talking to each other
b. good communication	**b.** different ideas about spending money
c. similar ideas about what is important	**c.** stressful jobs
d. _____	**d.** _____
e. _____	**e.** _____
f. _____	**f.** _____

Compare your answers with the class. Discuss why you think these things are important.

2. When people are in an unhappy marriage, what can they do? In your group think of some solutions for an unhappy marriage. Share your ideas with the class.

PREPARING TO LISTEN

A. BACKGROUND

Read the paragraph. Then follow the directions.

What makes a marriage happy? Some people say that love and trust are important. Others think that flexibility and friendship are most essential. Many people believe that good communication is necessary in order for a marriage to succeed. If two people are able to tell each other what they are thinking and feeling, they may be better able to work out solutions to their problems. Some people in the United States have even written marriage agreements to improve communication in their relationships. A marriage agreement is a written promise that is created by two people who are living together. In an agreement there are rules that tell how each partner in a relationship should behave. The rules differ depending on the priorities and personalities of the people writing the agreement.

Work in a small group. Read the quotations by famous people about marriage. Answer the questions. Then discuss the quotations with the class. Do you agree or disagree with the writers? Why or why not?

1. "In almost every marriage, there is a selfish and an unselfish partner. A pattern begins and never changes, of one person always asking for something and the other person always giving something away."

   Iris Murdoch, British writer and philosopher
   (b. 1919) [adapted]

   a. In most marriages, _____ can get what he or she wants.

      a. only one person

      b. both the husband and wife

      c. neither the husband nor the wife (no one)

   b. Does the writer have a positive or negative opinion of marriage?

   c. Does the writer feel that a husband and wife are equal or unequal in a marriage?

2. "A man who is a good friend is likely to find a good wife, because marriage is based on a talent for friendship."

Friedrich Nietzsche, German philosopher
(1844–1900) [adapted]

a. To have a happy marriage, a man must _____.

    a. have a good friend

    b. be a good friend to his wife

    c. be sure his wife has a good friend

b. Does the writer have a positive or negative opinion of marriage?

c. Does the writer feel that a husband and wife are equal or unequal in a marriage?

3. "A successful marriage is a house that must be rebuilt every day."

André Maurois, French writer and critic
(1885–1967) [adapted]

a. To have a successful marriage, a husband and wife must _____.

    a. work on their house

    b. build a nice house

    c. work to make each other happy

b. Does the writer have a positive or negative opinion of marriage?

c. Does the writer feel that a husband and wife are equal or unequal in a marriage?

B. VOCABULARY FOR COMPREHENSION

Read the conversations. Then choose the best words to complete the definitions of the underlined words.

1. A: Why are you angry with Brian?

   B: He brought a friend home for dinner without warning me. He's supposed to call first, but he always <u>breaks the rules</u> and just brings people over.

   To <u>break the rules</u> means to do something that is _____.

   a. not allowed   **b.** bad for you

2. A: Who is that <u>couple</u> over there?

   B: That's Bob Parsons and his wife, Jane.

   A <u>couple</u> is two people who are _____.

   a. married or dating   **b.** standing together

3. A: Do you want to <u>share</u> this cookie?

   B: Yes, you eat one half, and I'll eat the other half.

   To <u>share</u> means to _____.

   a. give something away   **b.** divide something into parts for each other

4. A: What are your <u>expectations</u> for marriage?

   B: I think we will be very happy and never argue.

   An <u>expectation</u> is a _____.

   a. hope or desire   **b.** past experience

5. A: Did Jane and Tomás bring their <u>spouses</u> to the party?

   B: Yes. Jane brought Bob. They've been married for ten years. And Tomás and Alissa got married last month.

   A <u>spouse</u> is a _____.

   a. friend   **b.** husband or wife

6. A: It really bothers me when my husband leaves his dirty socks on the floor. I can't stand it.

   B: I agree. That really <u>annoys</u> me, too.

   To <u>annoy</u> someone means to do something that makes the person feel _____.

   a. angry   b. happy

7. A: You know what my <u>pet peeve</u> is? When people smoke cigarettes in a restaurant.

   B: I hate it when people play loud music on the bus.

   A <u>pet peeve</u> is a(n) _____ that you dislike.

   a. person   b. action

8. A: How long did it take you to clean the house?

   B: I <u>spent a lot of time</u> cleaning. I think it took me three hours to finish.

   To <u>spend time</u> doing something means to _____.

   a. pay for someone's time   b. use time

9. A: You're late. Now we'll miss the movie.

   B: I'm sorry, honey. I <u>apologize</u>. I was stuck in traffic.

   To <u>apologize</u> means to say "_____."

   a. I'm sorry   b. I won't do it again

10. A: He was late, but he took me out to dinner to <u>make up for it</u>.

    B: That was nice. Did it make you feel better?

    To <u>make up for it</u> means to do something nice because you _____.

    a. did something wrong   b. feel like being nice

11. A: I'm feeling very, very angry right now!

    B: Why don't you go into the other room and <u>cool off</u>. We can talk when you feel less angry.

    To <u>cool off</u> means to become less _____.

    a. hot   **b.** angry

12. A: This list of phone numbers is five years old. I don't think it's correct anymore.

    B: You're right. I need to <u>update</u> the list.

    To <u>update</u> means to make something _____.

    a. newer or more current   **b.** longer or more complete

3 LISTENING ONE: A Marriage Agreement

A. INTRODUCING THE TOPIC

Listen to the announcer read the beginning of Bob and Jane Parsons' marriage agreement. Then listen to some questions the reporter asks later on in the interview. How do you think Bob and Jane will answer the questions?

1. Bob, Jane, first I'd like to ask you why you decided to write this unusual agreement?

   Predicted answer: _____

2. So, do you spend a lot of time checking to see if the other person is following the rules? Arguing?

   Predicted answer: _____

3. What happens if one of you breaks a rule?

   Predicted answer: _____

4. Do you think other couples should follow your example and write marriage agreements of their own?

   Predicted answer: _____

B. LISTENING FOR MAIN IDEAS

Listen to the interview. Several problems that married people have are discussed. Put a check next to the problems that are mentioned in the interview.

  √   **1.** working out day-to-day details and problems

_____ **2.** having different expectations than your spouse

_____ **3.** having problems with in-laws and family members

_____ **4.** not talking enough about what each person wants

_____ **5.** having disagreements about money

_____ **6.** being jealous about other men/women

_____ **7.** arguing

_____ **8.** not knowing how to apologize

_____ **9.** having disagreements about pets

C. LISTENING FOR DETAILS

Listen to the interview again. Listen for the details in the marriage agreement. Choose the correct letter to complete the statements.

1. HOUSEHOLD CHORES: _____ will do the household chores.

  a. Jane

  b. Bob

  c. Both Bob and Jane

2. GROCERY SHOPPING: Jane will always _____ when she shops for groceries.

  a. buy items on sale

  b. use a list

  c. spend less than $100 per week

3. CLEANING UP: Nothing will be left _____ overnight.

  a. on the kitchen table

  b. in the bedroom

  c. on the floor

4. SLEEPING: They will go to bed _____.

   a. at 11:00 P.M. every night

   b. at 11:00 P.M. on weeknights

   c. whenever they want to

5. CHILDREN: Bob and Jill will _____.

   a. wait five years before they have children

   b. have no more than three children

   c. both stop working to take care of the children

6. MONEY: Bob and Jane must both agree if one of them wants to spend _____.

   a. less than $100 dollars

   b. more than $100 dollars

   c. more than $200 dollars

7. COMMUNICATION: Bob and Jane must talk for fifteen to thirty minutes _____.

   a. every day

   b. every two days

   c. once a week

8. BREAKING THE RULES: If someone breaks the rules, they must apologize and _____.

   a. pay fifty dollars

   b. do something to make up for it

   c. never break the rule again

9. DRIVING: If they get lost in the car, they must ask for directions _____.

   a. after five minutes

   b. after driving for ten miles

   c. when they are far from home

10. ANGER: When they get angry, they must not _____.

   a. yell or use abusive language

   b. go into another room

   c. show their anger

11. CHANGING THE AGREEMENT: The marriage agreement must be updated _____.

   a. once a year

   b. every five years

   c. if they get divorced

D. LISTENING BETWEEN THE LINES

In the Background section on pages 183–184, you read some quotations by famous people about marriage. Read the following summaries of the quotations. Then listen to excerpts from the interview with Bob and Jane. Would Bob and Jane agree with the ideas in each summary? Circle **Yes** *or* **No**. *Then explain why you chose your answer. Use specific examples from the interview to show why they would agree or disagree.*

Excerpt 1

The quote by Iris Murdoch says that in most marriages only one person can get what he or she wants.

Would Bob and Jane agree with this idea?   Yes   No

Why or why not? _____

Excerpt 2

The quote by Friedrich Nietzsche says that to have a happy marriage, a man must be a good friend to his wife.

Would Bob and Jane agree with this idea?   Yes   No

Why or why not? _____

Excerpt 3

The quote by André Maurois says that to have a successful marriage, a husband and wife must work to make each other happy.

Would Bob and Jane agree with this idea?   Yes   No

Why or why not? _____

4 LISTENING TWO: Reactions to the Marriage Agreement

A. EXPANDING THE TOPIC

*Listen to people's reactions to Bob and Jane's marriage agreement. Do they think the agreement is a good idea or a bad idea? Listen for the speaker's opinion and check **Good idea** or **Bad idea**. Then draw a line to match the speaker with the reason for his or her opinion. One reason isn't mentioned.*

Speaker	Reason
Person 1: ❑ Good idea ❑ Bad idea	**a.** Makes couples think carefully before they marry
Person 2: ❑ Good idea ❑ Bad idea	**b.** Helps couples talk about problems
Person 3: ❑ Good idea ❑ Bad idea	**c.** Not romantic
Person 4: ❑ Good idea ❑ Bad idea	**d.** Not legal
	e. Too many details
Person 5: ❑ Good idea ❑ Bad idea	**f.** Divides household chores evenly.

B. LINKING LISTENINGS ONE AND TWO

Discuss these questions with the class.

1. What is your opinion of the marriage agreement between Bob and Jane? Do you agree or disagree with the comments made in Listening Two? Why or why not?

2. What would you do if you were about to get married and your future spouse asked you to write an agreement like Bob and Jane's?

3. What issues do you think two people should discuss before they live together?

5

REVIEWING LANGUAGE

A. EXPLORING LANGUAGE: Contrastive Stress

When we speak, we usually stress content words (nouns, verbs, adjectives, and adverbs). However, when we introduce new information into a conversation, we often emphasize different words to show that the new information contrasts with, or is different from, the old information. This kind of emphasis is called **contrastive stress.** By emphasizing, or stressing, different words in a sentence you can change the meaning.

Normal Sentence Stress Stress content words: ◆ nouns ◆ verbs ◆ adjectives ◆ adverbs	I **usually wash** the **dishes.**

Contrastive Stress
Stress words that add new information or contradict previous information.
	I usually wash the dishes.
	    (Not my wife.)
	I usually **wash** the dishes.
	    (Not dry them.)
	I usually wash the **dishes.**
	    (Not the car.)

To emphasize a word, say the word
    ◆ louder
    ◆ slower
    ◆ higher in pitch (tone)
	HE does the shopping.
	H-e-e does the shopping.
	
	He does the shopping.

1 *Listen to the tape or to your teacher reading the following sentences. Underline the word that is emphasized. Then circle **a** or **b** to choose the meaning of the sentence.*

1. Jane will do the grocery shopping.

   a. not Bob   **b.** not the laundry

2. Jane will always use a shopping list.

   a. not Bob   **b.** not sometimes

3. Nothing will be left on the floor in the bedroom.

   a. not the table   **b.** not the living room

4. We will go to bed at 11:00 P.M.

   a. not watch TV   **b.** not 9:00 P.M.

5. We will wait two years to have children.

   a. not three years   **b.** not two months

6. Bob and Jane can spend up to $100 dollars per week.

   a. not Jane only   **b.** not $200 dollars

7. We will spend thirty minutes a day talking with each other.

   a. not five minutes   **b.** not fighting

8. If we are driving and get lost, we will ask for directions.

   a. not walking   **b.** not for a map

9. If we get angry, we will go into separate rooms to cool off.

   a. not the same room   **b.** not to yell

10. Once a year, we will update this agreement.

    a. not twice a year   **b.** not throw it away

2 *Work in pairs. Student A chooses meaning **a** or **b** above and reads the sentences to Student B with the correct stress. Student B listens and guesses the meaning of the sentences. Then Students A and B change roles.*

B. WORKING WITH WORDS: Arguing and Apologizing

1 *Complete the paragraph below with the vocabulary from the listening.*

annoys	apologize	argue
cool off	expectations	get angry
pet peeves	share	spend a lot of time

My husband and I have different (**1**) _____ about who
will do the housework. I think we should (**2**) _____ the
cooking and cleaning, but he feels that I should do it all. One of my
(**3**) _____ is dirty dishes in the sink. Sometimes my
husband leaves dirty dishes in the sink. I feel like I
(**4**) _____ washing his dishes, instead of doing something else. It really (**5**) _____ me. I ask him to wash his
dishes, but he refuses. He doesn't think the problem is important.
Then I (**6**) _____. We (**7**) _____ about
the problem. Later, after we (**8**) _____ and don't feel
angry anymore, we both (**9**) _____ for getting angry.
But he still forgets to wash his dishes.

2 *In the interview Bob and Jane talked about what they do when they
have an argument. There are other words that have similar meanings
to the words in Exercise 1. Look at the words below. Write them in
the correct column.*

blow up	bug
calm down	do something to make up
fight	get on one's nerves
lose one's temper	quarrel
say you are sorry	compose oneself

annoy	get angry	argue	cool off	apologize
_____	_____	_____	_____	_____
_____	_____	_____	_____	_____

3 *Discuss your answers to these questions in a small group.*

1. Do you have any pet peeves that really get on your nerves? What do you do when something bugs you?

2. What makes you lose your temper. What do you do when you feel that you are going to blow up?

3. Who do you quarrel with the most? What do you usually fight about?

4. How do you calm down when you are angry?

5. Are you usually the first person to say you are sorry after an argument? What do you do to make up for getting angry?

6 SKILLS FOR EXPRESSION

A. GRAMMAR: Articles

1 *There are three **articles**: **a, an,** and **the**. Read the following section from Bob and Jane's agreement and underline the articles. Then answer the questions below.*

Article 12: Vacations. We will take a vacation every year. Most of the vacations will be in the United States, but once every five years, we will take an international trip. We will take turns deciding where to go. The person who decides will make the travel arrangements.

1. Look at the words that follow each article. Are they nouns, verbs, adjectives, or adverbs?

2. What is the difference between *a, an,* and *the?*

Articles

Articles are small words that come before nouns or noun phrases. They give information about whether a noun is specific or unspecific.

a. **The** is a definite (specific) article. Use **the** when:

◆ You and your listener both know which noun you are talking about

Bob broke **the** rule about asking for directions while driving.
(We know which rule he broke.)

◆ The noun is unique (there's only one)

Bob and Jane think that love is the only thing in **the** world that matters.
(There's only one world.)

◆ The noun has been mentioned already

Bob and Jane wrote a marriage agreement. **The** agreement outlines each person's responsibilities.
(We say "the agreement" because "agreement" was already mentioned in the first sentence.)

b. **A/an** is an indefinite (unspecific) article. Use **a/an** when:

◆ The noun is singular and
◆ Either you or your listener do not have a particular noun in mind

Jane will use **a** shopping list when she goes grocery shopping.
(We are talking about shopping lists in general, not a particular shopping list.)

Note: Use **a** before nouns that begin with a consonant sound and **an** before nouns that begin with a vowel sound.

Jane thinks **an** apology is better than **a** box of chocolates.

2 *Work in pairs. Read another section, which follows, from Bob and Jane's marriage agreement. Fill in the blanks with* **a, an,** *or* **the.** *Compare your answers with those of another pair and discuss any differences.*

Article 10a: Relatives. If **(1)** _____ family member comes to visit, **(2)** _____ person whose family is visiting will entertain **(3)** _____ visitor. **(4)** _____ other person will clean **(5)** _____ house. If either Bob or Jane has **(6)** _____ problem doing one of their jobs, they will discuss **(7)** _____ problem and perhaps switch roles for a while.

Article 10b: Relatives. If there is **(8)** _____ argument during **(9)** _____ family visit, **(10)** _____ person whose family is visiting will take responsibility for solving **(11)** _____ problem. Any solutions must be discussed privately between Bob and Jane before they are presented to **(12)** _____ family.

3 *Changing an article in a sentence can change the meaning of the sentence. Work in pairs. Student A chooses an article for each sentence and reads each sentence aloud. Student B listens and chooses the correct meaning* **a** *or* **b.** *Then switch: Student B reads and Student A chooses the meanings.*

Example

Jane needs to get a/the wedding dress.

a. She has chosen one and is going to pick it up.

b. She hasn't chosen one yet.

Student A: Jane needs to get the wedding dress.

Student B: The answer is (a).
(**The** shows that the speaker knows which dress Jane will get.)

Sentence

1. Bob wants a/the car.

2. Jane mailed a/the package.

Meaning

a. Bob doesn't have a car.

b. Bob wants to drive the car that he and Jane own.

a. I know which package she's mailing.

b. I don't know which package she's mailing.

3. Bob and Jane went to a/the movie on their anniversary.

a. The movie was "Love Story."

b. I don't know the title of the movie.

4. Bob and Jane are going to a/the wedding.

a. I know who's getting married.

b. I don't know who's getting married.

5. Jane bought Bob a/the shirt for his birthday.

a. I don't know what kind it was.

b. It was the green shirt that Bob had seen in the store the week before.

6. Jane had a/the talk with Bob.

a. Jane talked with Bob about something.

b. Jane had planned to talk with Bob about something, and she finally did.

7. Jane and Bob have an/the argument about once a month.

a. They always argue about the same thing.

b. They argue about different things.

8. Jane and Bob met at a/the movie theater.

a. There is only one movie theater in town.

b. There are several movie theaters.

B. STYLE: Interrupting to Take a Turn

❶ *When people participate in conversations or discussions they often interrupt each other. You can interrupt politely by learning when and how to interrupt. Look at the chart on page 199 for reasons for interrupting, when to interrupt, and the different ways to interrupt.*

Reasons for Interrupting

There are a number of reasons why a person might interrupt a conversation or discussion.

- To give an opinion
- To agree and add extra information
- To ask someone to repeat
- To disagree (argue) and explain why
- To ask someone to explain

When to Interrupt

It is important to interrupt at the appropriate time.

- When a speaker has finished his/her sentence
- When a speaker pauses in the middle of a sentence

How to Interrupt

There are different ways to interrupt. To interrupt politely you can do one or more of the following things or combine strategies.

Body Language (Sounds and Gestures)

- Clear your throat (say "uhmm")
- Raise your hand
- Raise your index finger
- Make eye contact with the speaker

Words/Phrases

- Excuse me, . . .
- I'm sorry. . . .
- Maybe so, but . . .
- Sorry to interrupt, but . . .

2 *Work in a small group. Choose a group leader. The leader begins a discussion on the following topic:*

> What things should you know about someone before you decide to live together?

Discuss this question for four minutes. During this time each person in the group should interrupt at least once using one or more of the strategies presented. As the group discusses, one student listens and uses the "Interruption Check Sheet" on page 200 to mark how each person interrupts. Each time a student interrupts, the listener puts a check (✓) in the appropriate column. At the end of the discussion, the listener shows the sheet to the group.

INTERRUPTION CHECK SHEET

Name of Student	Sounds/Gestures	Words
Example: Toby	✓✓✓	✓
1.		
2.		
3.		
4.		

3 *Arrange your chairs in a circle around the classroom. Stand next to your chair. The teacher or a student begins a discussion on the following question:*

Should people live together before they get married?

The discussion continues. Each time a student interrupts to take a turn, he/she can sit down. Once a student is sitting down, he/she can still participate but should give students who are still standing opportunities to speak. The discussion ends when everybody is sitting down.

Note: If there are more than twenty students in the class, divide into two groups before proceeding with the activity.

ON YOUR OWN

A. SPEAKING TOPIC: Writing a Marriage Agreement

You have been hearing about Bob and Jane's marriage agreement. If you were to write a similar agreement, what would you include in it? Work in a small group to write an agreement that includes rules for people who want to live together.

a. Divide into groups.

b. Choose a writer and a speaker for your group.

c. Look at the marriage agreement below. It lists three topics that people often argue about when they live together. Add a fourth topic. Then write at least three rules for each topic. As you discuss, the writer writes the group's ideas on a large piece of paper. (During the discussion everyone should use interruption strategies to speak at least once [see Section 6B].)

d. Check your agreement for spelling and grammar. (Pay special attention to articles [see Section 6A].)

✳ *Marriage Agreement* ✳

A. Housework

1. _____
   _____
   _____

2. _____
   _____
   _____

3. _____
   _____
   _____

C. Money

1. _____
   _____
   _____

2. _____
   _____
   _____

3. _____
   _____
   _____

B. Employment

1. _____
   _____
   _____

2. _____
   _____
   _____

3. _____
   _____
   _____

D. _____

1. _____
   _____
   _____

2. _____
   _____
   _____

3. _____
   _____
   _____

Presentation

Put your group's agreement on a classroom wall. The speaker for each group presents his/her group's agreement.

Listening Task

After each group has presented, be prepared to discuss the following:

a. What problems are these rules trying to solve?
b. Does your group have any rules that are different from the ones presented? If so, what are they?

B. FIELDWORK

1. ORAL HISTORY

Interview a married couple. Ask them to tell the story of how they met. Here are some questions to help you get the conversation going:

a. When were you married?
b. How did you meet? (Where was it? What did you think of each other?)
c. How did this first meeting lead to marriage?

Take notes during the interview. Then make a tape recording of the story. Speak for three minutes. Don't write out the story ahead of time. Use your notes and speak clearly and naturally.

2. RESEARCH

Go to the library and look up one of the following marriage topics in an encyclopedia or on the Internet.

no-fault divorce	covenant marriage	polygamy
civil ceremony	same-sex marriage	_____ (your choice)
annulment	domestic partnership	

Use these questions to help you with your research:

a. What is _____?

b. In what cultures might you find _____?

c. Would _____ be acceptable in your culture? Why or why not?

d. What do you think about _____? Why do you feel this way?

Meet in a small group with students who chose a different topic from you. Present your research and discuss your opinions.

STUDENT ACTIVITIES

UNIT 6 ◆ WORKING WITH AIDS PATIENTS

EXERCISE 2, page 111

Student B

Read the story about a nurse who worked in an AIDS ward. Write questions below to find out the missing information from your partner. (The first question is done for you.) Answer your partner's questions. Then, ask your partner your questions and fill in the information.

Mary Salinger started working as a nurse in the AIDS ward at San Francisco University Hospital on June 1, (1) _____. The next year, at three o'clock in the morning on New Year's Eve, she saw a terrible accident while she was working in (2) _____. While Mary was giving a patient an injection, the doctor she was working with accidentally pricked his hand on the bloody needle. Three months later, the doctor took an HIV test because (3) _____. The test showed that the doctor had the HIV virus. Mary felt very upset about the accident and the infection of the doctor. Then, two weeks later, she found out that the accident didn't have to happen. (4) _____ told her that there was a special type of needle that had a protective cover. Mary thought, "This is great! We'll never have an accident with a needle again!" She asked the director of the hospital to order the safe type of needles. He said no, he couldn't order them because (5) _____. Mary was very angry. She felt that (6) _____ was more important than saving money.

Questions

1. <u>What year did Mary Salinger start working as a nurse</u> _____?
2. _____?
3. _____?
4. _____?
5. _____?
6. _____?

UNIT 7 ◆ ENGINE TROUBLE

EXERCISE 2, page 129

Student B

1. *Listen to Student A read the story. After each sentence, choose a vocabulary word to complete each sentence below. Read the sentence aloud. Your partner will tell you if you are correct. (Try not to look back at the word list!)*

   a. You _____ with your coworker, right?

   b. He thought the roads were _____, right?

   c. He couldn't _____ the car, right?

   d. He tried to _____ the car, right?

   e. You told him not to stop _____ on the ice, right?

   f. You had a big _____, right?

   g. Next time, you think you should _____, right?

2. *Read the sentences of the story to Student A one by one. Wait for Student A to check the information by using a new vocabulary word. Tell your partner if the sentence is correct or not.*

   a. I had to buy a new car, but I didn't know what kind of car or truck I wanted. (Answer: *vehicle*)

   b. I wanted a car that looks stylish and fashionable. (Answer: *cool*)

   c. I chose a four-wheel drive pickup truck, but my friend says that is a very bad choice. (Answer: *terrible*)

   d. He says that I don't need that car because I live just outside the city. (Answer: *suburbs*)

   e. He says that four-wheel drive really reduces the gas mileage. (Answer: *cuts down on*)

   f. I don't need to carry things, so he says a pickup truck is not very useful for me. (Answer: *practical*)

   g. He says I'm stupid for choosing the pickup truck. (Answer: *dummy*)

UNIT 9 ◆ TO SPANK OR NOT TO SPANK?

EXERCISE 2, page 168

Student B, Part 1

Listen to Student A read sentences 1–10. Read the sentences below back to your partner, filling in the space with a word with a prefix. Your sentence should have the same meaning as the sentence Student A reads to you. Your partner will tell you if your answer is correct.

1. Children _____ getting punished.

2. Doctors recommend punishment that is _____.

3. Hitting a child is an _____ type of punishment.

4. What did she say? I _____.

5. The boy _____ his teacher.

6. Good grades in school are _____ to my daughter.

7. The children _____ today.

8. This airplane flies _____ to Hawaii.

9. Some children are _____ to their parents.

10. I think spanking is _____.

Part 2

Read sentences 11–20 to Student A. Your partner will repeat the sentences, changing the underlined words to a word with a prefix. Tell your partner if his or her answer is correct. (The correct answers are in parentheses.)

11. Violent behavior is <u>not acceptable</u>. (unacceptable)

12. He is <u>not friendly</u>. (unfriendly)

13. I always <u>pronounce</u> that word <u>badly</u>. (mispronounce)

14. I like beer that is <u>made without alcohol</u>. (nonalcoholic)

15. Ice cream <u>without fat</u> is healthier. (nonfat)

16. Many parents <u>don't approve</u> of spanking. (disapprove)

17. I <u>don't like</u> punishing my children. (dislike)

18. Parents <u>don't agree</u> about spanking. (disagree)

19. She <u>didn't use</u> her computer <u>correctly</u>, so it broke. (misused)

20. We teach children that hitting other people is <u>not kind</u>. (unkind)

ANSWER KEY

UNIT 1 ◆
ADVERTISING ON THE AIR

2B. VOCABULARY FOR COMPREHENSION

1. d	3. j	5. h	7. i	9. b
2. a	4. c	6. e	8. g	10. f

3B. LISTENING FOR MAIN IDEAS

1 1. Humor   Doggie's Friend Flea Collar
    2. Thriftiness   Benton's Furniture
    3. Ego   Younger You Hair Color
2 1. b   2. a   3. b

3C. LISTENING FOR DETAILS

1. b	3. a	5. c	7. b	9. c
2. a	4. c	6. a	8. a	10. a

4A. EXPANDING THE TOPIC

   _a_ Ad 1   _c_ Ad 2   _b_ Ad 3

5A. EXPLORING LANGUAGE: Sentence Stress

1 **a.** KATHY: Hello?
      LIZ: <u>Kathy</u>! I took your <u>advice</u>.
      KATHY: <u>What</u> advice?
      LIZ: I colored my <u>hair</u>.
      KATHY: With <u>Younger You</u>?
      LIZ: <u>Yes</u>! It's <u>great</u>!
   b. KATHY: Did you hear about the sale at <u>Benton's</u>?
      LIZ: <u>Yes</u>, I'm going <u>today</u>. How about <u>you</u>?
      KATHY: I think I'll stop by <u>tomorrow</u>.

5B. WORKING WITH WORDS: Word Forms

1

Noun	Verb	Adjective
1. advertisement/ advertising	advertise	X
2. emotion	X	emotional
3. influence	influence	influential
4. appeal	appeal	appealing
5. X	humor	humorous
6. thriftiness/thrift	X	thrifty
7. speciality	specialize	special specialized
8. ego	X	egotistical
9. creation	create	creative
10. product	produce	productive

2 1. product   2. humorous   3. advertisement
    4. advertisements 5. influence 6. advertised 7. appealing
    8. creative 9. emotions 10. special 11. thrifty
    12. egotistical

3 1. humorous   6. thrifty
    2. produced   7. creative
    3. special   8. emotional
    4. influential   9. appealing
    5. advertisements   10. egos

6B. STYLE: Giving Instructions

1 Order of steps: 2, 1, 4, 5, 3

UNIT 2 ◆
TRAVELING THROUGH TIME ZONES

2B. VOCABULARY FOR COMPREHENSION

1. b	3. a	5. a	7. a	9. b
2. b	4. b	6. b	8. a	10. a

3B. LISTENING FOR MAIN IDEAS

1. T	3. T	5. F
2. F	4. F	6. T

3C. LISTENING FOR DETAILS

1. a	3. b	5. c	7. b	9. c
2. c	4. b	6. c	8. a	10. a

4A. EXPANDING THE TOPIC

1. a	2. e	3. f	4. b	5. d

5A. EXPLORING LANGUAGE: Syllable Stress

1

_3_ ad/van/tage	_2_ play/er
_3_ dif/fi/cult	_2_ prob/lem
_4_ dis/ad/van/tage	_2_ rec/ords
_2_ doc/tor	_3_ re/sear/cher
_2_ ef/fect	_2_ se/ries
_2_ head/aches	_2_ short/er
_3_ hos/pi/tal	_2_ symp/tom
_2_ mea/sure	_2_ tired/ness
	_2_ trou/ble

UNIT 3 ◆
TOO GOOD TO BE TRUE

2B. VOCABULARY FOR COMPREHENSION

a. 7	c. 2	e. 9	g. 10	i. 5
b. 4	d. 1	f. 6	h. 8	j. 3

3B. LISTENING FOR MAIN IDEAS

Order of Ideas: 6, 2, 4, 1, 5, 3

3C. LISTENING FOR DETAILS

1. a	3. b	5. a	7. b	9. a
2. b	4. a	6. a	8. b	10. a

3D. LISTENING BETWEEN THE LINES

1 Steps in the Con Game: 3, 1, 5, 2, 4

4A. EXPANDING THE TOPIC

1. d	2. b	3. a	4. c

5A. EXPLORING LANGUAGE: Reductions

Part 2

1 A: Hello, Ma'am? Congratulations! You're <u>gonna</u> be rich! I have some exciting prizes for you.

    B: Really? What do I <u>hafta</u> do?

A: Well, first I <u>hafta</u> ask you this. Which prize do you <u>wanna</u> get: the luxury car or ten thousand dollars?

B: I <u>wanna</u> get a new car, but I'd also like some money. Can I have both?

A: No, I'm sorry. You <u>hafta</u> choose one of them.

B: Hold on. I'm <u>gonna</u> ask my husband which one he wants! . . . OK, I'm back. He says he wants to get the money.

A: Great! Now, to get the prize, you <u>hafta</u> send a small deposit of five hundred dollars.

B: OK. I'm going to the bank this afternoon, so I can get the money.

5B. WORKING WITH WORDS: Impossible Sentences

❶ Answers may vary. Suggested answers:

1. a lie	**6.** prize
2. more	**7.** police
3. quick	**8.** dishonest
4. trusted	**9.** doesn't know
5. believed everything	**10.** are

UNIT 4 ◆
IF YOU CAN'T BEAT 'EM, JOIN 'EM

2B. VOCABULARY FOR COMPREHENSION

1. h	**3.** e	**5.** b	**7.** g	**9.** a
2. d	**4.** j	**6.** f	**8.** c	**10.** i

3B. LISTENING FOR MAIN IDEAS

Order of Ideas: 7, 4, 5, 2, 1, 3, 6

3C. LISTENING FOR DETAILS

1. a	**3.** b	**5.** a	**7.** c	**9.** c
2. b	**4.** a	**6.** c	**8.** a	**10.** b

4A. EXPANDING THE TOPIC

❶ Eat dead skin on an injury - Maggots - In a hospital - TRUE

Bring medicine to people - Mosquitoes - Far away from doctors - FALSE

Used in medical tests - Fireflies - In a scientific laboratory - TRUE

Add protein to food - Termites - In poor countries - TRUE

5A. EXPLORING LANGUAGE: Plural *S*

❶ /S/

ants	crickets	maggots	termites

/Z/

spiders	butterflies	fireflies	bees
ladybugs	mosquitoes		

/IZ/

cockroaches	praying mantises

5B. WORKING WITH WORDS

❶ Explanations will vary.

2. learn	**4.** failure	**6.** keep	**8.** building
3. find out	**5.** stupid	**7.** insect	**9.** science

❷ **Cause : Effect**

1. breed : babies
2. feed : live
3. exterminate : die
4. collect : together

Opposite

1. advantage : disadvantage
2. pick up : put down
3. predictable : unpredictable
4. dangerous : safe

Part : Whole

2. apple : fruit
3. fly swatter : extermination method
4. kitchen : house

6A. GRAMMAR: Infinitives of Purpose

❷ **2.** e
3. i
4. g
5. a
6. c
7. d
8. f
9. h

2. He used a fly swatter (in order) to get rid of the fireflies.

3. He went to the park in the springtime (in order) to see the butterflies.

4. He opened his window at night (in order) to hear the crickets singing.

5. He put some cream on his arms in order not to get mosquito bites.

6. He cleaned the corner of his ceiling in order not to have any spider webs.

7. He cleaned all the food off the kitchen table in order not to leave any food for the ants.

8. He put some ladybugs in his garden (in order) to stop other insects from eating his plants.

9. He kept a hive full of bees in the garden (in order) to make honey.

UNIT 5 ◆
UNDERSTANDING ACCENTS

2B. VOCABULARY FOR COMPREHENSION

❷ **a.** 6	**c.** 1	**e.** 4	**g.** 7	**i.** 8
b. 2	**d.** 5	**f.** 9	**h.** 3	**j.** 10

3B. LISTENING FOR MAIN IDEAS

Order of Topics: 4, 1, 5, 6, 3, 2

3C. LISTENING FOR DETAILS

1. b	**3.** b	**5.** a	**7.** a	**9.** b
2. a	**4.** b	**6.** b	**8.** a	**10.** b

4A. EXPANDING THE TOPIC

1. a	**2.** b	**3.** a	**4.** b

5A. EXPLORING LANGUAGE: Question Intonation

1.
1. rising
2. falling
3. rising
4. falling
5. falling
6. rising
7. rising
8. rising
9. falling

5B. WORKING WITH WORDS: Phrasal Verbs

1.
1. b, a
2. a, b
3. b, a
4. b, a
5. b, a
6. b, a
7. a, b

2.
2. up
3. up
4. on
5. up
6. out
7. about
8. by

UNIT 6 ◆
WORKING WITH AIDS PATIENTS

2A. BACKGROUND

2. Suggested answers:
1. no
2. no
3. no
4. no
5. maybe
6. no
7. no
8. no
9. maybe
10. maybe

2B. VOCABULARY FOR COMPREHENSION

1. a
2. b
3. b
4. a
5. b
6. a
7. a
8. a
9. b
10. b
11. a
12. b

3B. LISTENING FOR MAIN IDEAS

1. a
2. c
3. a
4. b
5. b
6. c

3C. LISTENING FOR DETAILS

1. T
2. F
3. T
4. T
5. T
6. F
7. F
8. T
9. T
10. F

4A. EXPANDING THE TOPIC

a. Call 1, not possible
b. Call 3, possible
c. Call 2, not possible

5A. EXPLORING LANGUAGE: *CAN/CAN'T*

1. can't
2. can
3. can
4. can't
5. can't
6. can
7. can't
8. can
9. can
10. can't

6A. GRAMMAR: *Wh-* Questions—Subject and Predicate

2. *Student A: Questions*

2. When/What time did Mary see the accident?

3. What was Mary doing when the doctor accidentally pricked his hand?

4. How did Mary feel about the accident and the infection of the doctor?

5. What did the special type of needle have?

6. Who did Mary ask to order the safe type of needles?

Student B: Questions

2. Where was Mary working when she saw the terrible accident?

3. Why did the doctor take an HIV test?

4. Who told her there was a special type of needle?

5. Why couldn't the director order the safe type of needle?

6. What was more important than saving money?

UNIT 7 ◆
ENGINE TROUBLE

2B. VOCABULARY FOR COMPREHENSION

1. b
2. b
3. b
4. a
5. a
6. b
7. a
8. b
9. a
10. a

3B. LISTENING FOR MAIN IDEAS

1. c
2. b
3. c
4. a
5. b

3C. LISTENING FOR DETAILS

1. Frank
2. Bob or Roy
3. Frank's wife
4. Frank's wife
5. Bob or Roy
6. Bob or Roy
7. Bob's wife
8. Bob or Roy
9. Bob or Roy
10. Bob or Roy

3D. LISTENING BETWEEN THE LINES

Part 1
1. c
2. b
3. d
4. a

Part 2
5. f
6. h
7. e
8. g

4A. EXPANDING THE TOPIC

Call 1   b
Call 2   a
Call 3   c

5A. EXPLORING LANGUAGE: Intonation

1.
1. Right?
2. Right.
3. OK?
4. OK.
5. Right?
6. Right.
7. OK?
8. OK.

5B. WORKING WITH WORDS: Paraphrasing

1.
1. suburb
2. vehicle
3. cut down on
4. steer
5. keep your mouth shut
6. carpool
7. cool
8. argument
9. suddenly
10. brake
11. dummy
12. dry
13. practical
14. terrible
15. gas mileage

6A. GRAMMAR: Future Tense

2.
1. Will cars be smaller? *or* Are cars going to be smaller?

2. Will people drive less than they do now? *or* Are people going to drive less than they do now?

3. Will cars be more expensive? *or* Are cars going to be more expensive?

4. Will traffic be worse? *or* Is traffic going to be worse?

5. What type of car will be the most popular? *or* What type of car is going to be the most popular?

6. Will cars run on gas or electricity? *or* Are cars going to run on gas or electricity?

7. What new options will cars have? *or* What new options are cars going to have?

8. What types of problems will cars cause in the future? *or* What types of problems are cars going to cause in the future?

9. Will you own a car in the future? *or* Are you going to own a car in the future?

UNIT 8 ◆
YOU ARE WHAT YOU WEAR

2B. VOCABULARY FOR COMPREHENSION

1. l	4. a	7. i	10. b
2. g	5. h	8. k	11. f
3. d	6. c	9. e	12. j

3B. LISTENING FOR MAIN IDEAS

Part 1
Topics mentioned: 1, 2, 4, 6, 7, 9

Part 2

1. a	2. b	3. a

3C. LISTENING FOR DETAILS

1. T	3. T	5. F	7. T	9. T
2. F	4. F	6. T	8. F	10. T

4A. EXPANDING THE TOPIC

1. b	2. c	3. c	4. c	5. b

6. No, because he feels strange.

5A. EXPLORING LANGUAGE: Thought Groups

❷ 2. a-d, b-c   5. a-d, b-c   7. a-c, b-d
3. a-c, b-d   6. a-d, b-c   8. a-d, b-c
4. a-d, b-c

5B. WORKING WITH WORDS: Analogies

❶ 1. Sri Lanka   4. modern
2. old-fashioned   5. independent
3. sari   6. Britain

UNIT 9 ◆
TO SPANK OR NOT TO SPANK?

2B. VOCABULARY FOR COMPREHENSION

a. 8	d. 9	g. 4	j. 12
b. 5	e. 7	h. 1	k. 6
c. 3	f. 2	i. 10	l. 11

3B. LISTENING FOR MAIN IDEAS

Answers in the "Reason(s)" section may vary.
1. Dale Clover supports spanking.

2. Rhonda Moore supports spanking.

3. Taylor Robinson opposes spanking.

4. Dr. John Oparah supports spanking.

5. Dr. Beverly Lau opposes spanking.

3C. LISTENING FOR DETAILS

1. Y	4. N	7. Y	10. N
2. Y	5. Y	8. N	11. N
3. N	6. N	9. Y	12. Y

4A. EXPANDING THE TOPIC

Answers in the "Reason(s)" section may vary.
1. Donald Sterling opposes spanking. Reason: Children who are spanked often grow up to be criminals.

2. Dr. Phyllis Jones supports spanking. Reason: Teenagers did better when they had clear discipline as children; Spanking doesn't hurt children.

3. Dr. Armando Mazzone opposes spanking. Spanking can cause serious health problems, such as back injury.

4. Lois Goldin supports spanking. The number of parents who spank is going down, but the amount of violent crime is rising.

5A. EXPLORING LANGUAGE: Prefixes

❶ 1. unacceptable   9. dislike
2. disobeys   10. mispronounces
3. misuses   11. disrespectful
4. nonfat   12. nonstop
5. disapprove   13. misunderstands
6. unfriendly   14. unimportant
7. misbehaves   15. nonalcoholic
8. unkind

5B. WORKING WITH WORDS: Stronger vs. Weaker Language

	Stronger word	Weaker word	Word that doesn't belong
1.	beat	spank	reward
2.	abuse	be unkind to	take care of
3.	respect	like	remember
4.	violent	rough	gentle
5.	misbehave	make a mistake	are good
6.	abusive	aggressive	quiet
7.	terrible	serious	positive
8.	angry	annoyed	calm
9.	debate	talk about	agree about
10.	oppose	disagree with	support

6A. GRAMMAR: Present Perfect

❷ 1. have stopped
2. has passed, have arrested
3. have advised, have suggested
4. has risen, haven't taught
5. have stopped, has decided
❸ 1. have . . . changed
2. has . . . passed
3. have . . . advised
4. Have . . . risen . . . fallen
5. has . . . changed

UNIT 10 ◆
A MARRIAGE AGREEMENT

2B. VOCABULARY FOR COMPREHENSION

1. a	4. a	7. b	10. a
2. a	5. b	8. b	11. b
3. b	6. a	9. a	12. a

3B. LISTENING FOR MAIN IDEAS

Topics mentioned: 1, 2, 4, 5, 7, 8

3C. LISTENING FOR DETAILS

1. c	4. b	7. a	10. a
2. b	5. b	8. b	11. a
3. c	6. b	9. a	

4A. EXPANDING THE TOPIC

Person 1: Bad idea. Reason: c

Person 2: Bad idea. Reason: e

Person 3: Good idea. Reason: b

Person 4: Bad idea. Reason: d

Person 5: Good idea. Reason: a

5A. EXPLORING LANGUAGE: Contrastive Stress

1 1. a   4. b   7. b   9. a

2. b   5. a   8. a   10. b

3. b   6. a

5B. WORKING WITH WORDS: Arguing and Apologizing

1 1. expectations   6. get angry

2. share   7. argue

3. pet peeves   8. cool off

4. spend a lot of time   9. apologize

5. annoys

2 **annoy:** bug, get on one's nerves

get angry: blow up, lose one's temper

argue: fight, quarrel

cool off: calm down, compose oneself

apologize: say you are sorry, do something to make up

6A. GRAMMAR: Articles

2 1. a   5. the   9. a

2. the   6. a   10. the

3. the   7. the   11. the

4. The   8. an   12. the

3 1. **a.** a car   5. **a.** a shirt

    b. the car   **b.** the shirt

2. **a.** the package   6. **a.** a talk

    b. a package   **b.** the talk

3. **a.** the movie   7. **a.** the argument

    b. a movie   **b.** an argument

4. **a.** the wedding   8. **a.** the movie theater

    b. a wedding   **b.** a movie theater

TAPESCRIPT

UNIT 1 ◆ ADVERTISING ON THE AIR

3. LISTENING ONE: Advertising on the Air

A. *Introducing the Topic*

① **Professor:** Good morning, class! As you remember, last week we talked about the history of radio advertising. Today we're going to start talking about how radio advertisers use our emotions to get us to buy the products they're selling.

② **ADVERTISEMENT 1**

Speaker: It's flea season again! Fleas! Those pesky insects jump into your dog's hair, bite his skin, make him itch. . . .

ADVERTISEMENT 2

Voices: 10-9-8-7. . . .

Speaker: It's a countdown time!

Voices: . . . 6-5-4. . . .

ADVERTISEMENT 3

Liz: It's amazing! You really <u>do</u> look younger!

Kathy: Thanks! Now people don't believe I'm a grandmother.

B. *Listening for Main Ideas*

Professor: Good morning class! As you remember, last week we talked about the history of radio advertising. Today we're going to start talking about how radio advertisers use our emotions to get us to buy the products they're selling. There are so many emotions that advertisements try to influence. To affect a particular emotion, advertisers make what we call an emotional appeal. Today I'm going to talk about three appeals that are often used to influence us to buy. I think you'll find it interesting because I've brought with me some real live radio ads to play for you as examples. . . . OK, let's get started.

One of the most popular emotional appeals that advertisers use is the appeal to humor. We all like to hear funny stories, so by making an ad humorous, the advertisers hope that we'll remember it and will, therefore, remember the product. Let me play for you an example of a humorous ad. This is for a product that you can use to get rid of your dog's fleas. OK! Here's the ad. . . .

Speaker: It's flea season again! Fleas! Those pesky insects jump into your dog's hair, bite his skin, make him itch. Unfortunately, most flea treatments involve bathing with harsh chemicals. It wasn't fun for me or my dog. That's why I'm getting the "Doggie's Friend" flea collar. It goes around your dog's neck and makes a noise that drives fleas crazy. . . . So off they jump! When I used the collar last season, my dog was flea-free in five minutes!

Announcer: Don't delay. Get a "Doggie's Friend" today.

Professor: Well . . . obviously the man's very happy with his "Doggie's Friend" collar. You probably noticed the humorous

doggie noises in the background. They're cute and funny, which helps us remember the ad. Even the name of the collar—"Doggie's Friend"—is kind of cute, so the humor seems to fit the product. That brings up a key point, which is the importance of fitting the right emotional appeal with the right product. In the case of humor, it wouldn't really be appropriate to make a funny ad for a serious product. Like . . . say . . . a law firm that specializes in divorce. You wouldn't want to use humor to advertise that.

All right, now let's talk about another appeal—the appeal to thriftiness. By thriftiness I'm talking about the desire to save money. Most shoppers are more likely to buy something if it's on sale than if it's full price. The following ad is for a furniture store that's having a big sale. Notice how the ad gets the listener to focus on the low prices. OK! Here we go. . . .

Voices: 10-9-8-7. . . .

Speaker: It's countdown time!

Voices: . . . 6-5-4. . . .

Speaker: Only a few more seconds until Benton's Furniture opens its doors for its annual clearance sale! Save big on dining room furniture! Dining tables 50% off! Save big on living room furniture! . . . So hurry before it's . . .

Voices: . . . 3-2-1. . . .

Speaker: . . . too late!

Announcer: Benton's Furniture. 142 Willow Creek Road.

Professor: OK. It's not hard to see that Benton's main attraction is its low prices. In fact, the ad talks only about prices and not about the quality of the furniture or what the store specializes in. Notice also the use of the countdown technique. As the actor counts down from 10 to 1 it makes us feel that we should hurry to Benton's before everything gets sold.

All right. . . . The last kind of ad is the advertisement that appeals to our egos. Our egos make us do things to look good in front of others. For example, we might buy a luxury car to look rich, or we might join a health club to get in shape . . . all because we want to look good. This desire is so strong that advertisers often create ads that speak to our egos. Here's one such ad. It's for a hair care product. As you listen, focus on this question: How does this product make you look better?

Liz: Hi, Kathy! . . . Say . . . did you do something to your hair?

Kathy: Yup! I colored it with a new product called "Younger You."

Liz: It's amazing! You really <u>do</u> look younger!

Kathy: Thanks. Now people don't believe I'm a grandmother.

Liz: I should try it.

Kathy: It's so easy to use. Just mix it with your shampoo, wash, and rinse.

Liz: Sounds great!

Announcer: Only five minutes to a younger you.

Professor: OK. So how does this product make you look better? . . . Yes, Linda. . . .

Linda: It colors gray hair.

Professor: Right! Notice the use of the admiring friend who tells Kathy how great she looks. That's the appeal to ego. Appeal to ego is a really popular advertising technique. You'll often see it being used to sell products that improve your appearance, like cosmetics and weight-loss programs.

OK! That's it for today's lecture. We'll continue talking about some other appeals tomorrow. Are there any questions at this point? . . . . (voice fades out)

C. *Listening for Details*

(repeat Section 3B)

D. *Listening between the Lines*

ADVERTISEMENT 1

Speaker: It's flea season again! Fleas! Those pesky insects jump into your dog's hair, bite his skin, make him itch. Unfortunately, most flea treatments involve bathing with harsh chemicals. It wasn't fun for me or my dog. That's why I'm getting the "Doggie's Friend" flea collar. It goes around your dog's neck and makes a noise that drives fleas crazy. . . . So off they jump! When I used the collar last season, my dog was flea-free in five minutes!

Announcer: Don't delay. Get a "Doggie's Friend" today.

ADVERTISEMENT 2

Voices: 10-9-8-7. . . .

Speaker: It's countdown time!

Voices: . . . 6-5-4. . . .

Speaker: Only a few more seconds until Benton's Furniture opens its doors for its annual clearance sale! Save big on dining room furniture! Dining tables 50% off! Save big on living room furniture! . . . So hurry before it's . . .

Voices: . . . 3-2-1. . . .

Speaker: . . . too late!

Announcer: Benton's Furniture. 142 Willow Creek Road.

ADVERTISEMENT 3

Liz: Hi, Kathy! . . . Say. . . did you do something to your hair?

Kathy: Yup! I colored it with a new product called "Younger You."

Liz: It's amazing! You really <u>do</u> look younger!

Kathy: Thanks. Now people don't believe I'm a grandmother.

Liz: I should try it.

Kathy: It's so easy to use. Just mix it with your shampoo, wash, and rinse.

Liz: Sounds great!

Announcer: Only five minutes to a younger you.

4. LISTENING TWO: Other Appeals

A. *Expanding the Topic*

ADVERTISEMENT 1

Speaker: You park your car, and your worst nightmare happens! When you come back . . . it's gone! It can happen anywhere . . . at the store, at work, even outside your own house! It can happen to anyone, and chances are, it will happen to YOU! That's why Murphy's Car Products designed the incredible "Thief Buster" security system. It's easy to use and 100% effective. Just press the "on" button when you leave your car. If someone touches your car while you're away, a loud bell will ring. And if that doesn't stop the thief, the engine will automatically cut off when he starts the car. So why put your car at risk any longer? Get a "Thief Buster" security system today! "Thief Buster". . . protection for your peace of mind!

ADVERTISEMENT 2

Speaker: It's 11:00 A.M. You sink your tired body into the soft, white sand and feel the warm sun beating on your back . . . melting away all tension . . . clearing your mind. The only sounds you hear are the cries of birds . . . far away . . . and the clink of the ice in your cool tropical punch. You reach for a piece of sweet, juicy pineapple as you make your biggest decision of the day. . . . What will I have for lunch?

Announcer: Escape to relaxing Hawaii. Call "Tropical Hawaiian Vacations" at 1(800)333-4445. "Tropical Hawaiian Vacations" . . . your ticket to paradise.

ADVERTISEMENT 3

Mother: Hi, kids! How was school?

Girl & Boy: Fine!

Girl: How was work?

Mother: Busy, busy, busy!

Boy: What's for dinner? I have soccer practice at 7:00.

Mother: Soccer! Oh no! I completely forgot! Let's see . . . what can we make?

Girl: How about a Clayton's dinner?

Mother: Great idea!

Announcer: Clayton's dinners are perfect for today's busy families. They're made of healthy ingredients with very little fat and no preservatives. And they're delicious, too. Choose from chicken teriyaki, lasagna, beef pot pie, and dozens of other dishes. So good. So easy. Just pop them in the microwave, 15 minutes, and they're ready to go!

Boy: Hmmm! This is great Mom!

Girl: We should eat like this every night!

Announcer: "Clayton's Dinners." So good. So easy.

5. REVIEWING LANGUAGE

A. *Exploring Language: Sentence Stress*

Liz: It's <u>amazing</u>! You really <u>do</u> look younger!

Kathy: <u>Thanks</u>. Now people don't believe I'm a <u>grandmother</u>.

Liz: <u>I</u> should try it.

1. Kathy: Hello?

Liz: <u>Kathy</u>! I took your <u>advice</u>.

Kathy: <u>What</u> advice?

Liz: I colored my <u>hair</u>.

Kathy: With <u>Younger You</u>?

Liz: <u>Yes</u>! It's <u>great</u>!

2. Kathy: Did you hear about the sale at <u>Benton's</u>?

Liz: <u>Yes</u>, I'm going <u>today</u>. How about <u>you</u>?

Kathy: I think I'll stop by <u>tomorrow</u>.

UNIT 2 ◆ TRAVELING THROUGH TIME ZONES

3. LISTENING ONE: News Report

A. *Introducing the Topic*

Kate: With thousands of people traveling every day as a part of their jobs, there is great concern about the effect of jet lag on business travelers. In the world of international business, many men and women have trouble performing their jobs because they feel tired and sick from all their traveling. Businesspeople are not the only professionals who suffer from jet lag. Professional sports players also find that jet lag affects their performance. In today's health report, Jim Hernandez looks at the problem of jet lag in professional baseball. Baseball and jet lag, what's the connection, Jim?

B. *Listening for Main Ideas*

Kate: With thousands of people traveling every day as a part of their jobs, there is great concern about the effect of jet lag on business travelers. In the world of international business, many men and women have trouble performing their jobs because they feel tired and sick from all their traveling. Businesspeople are not the only professionals who suffer from jet lag. Professional sports players also find that jet lag affects their performance. In today's health report, Jim Hernandez looks at the problem of jet lag in professional baseball. Baseball and jet lag, what's the connection, Jim?

Jim: Well, Kate, this news may be of interest to all of us, not just baseball fans. You see, researchers have wondered about how jet lag affects the job performance of people who travel for a living. The problem is that it is very difficult to measure exactly how jet lag affects most travelers—how can we measure the performance of, say, an executive who travels to another country to make a business deal? This is where the idea of looking at baseball comes in. We can measure the performance of baseball players, so by looking at whether baseball teams win or lose games, researchers believe that we can see how jet lag affects performance in sports, business, and other jobs.

The study, released today, focuses on the performance of professional baseball teams. It looks at the number of games won or lost by teams after they travel to another city to play a baseball game. In the study, doctors from the University of Massachusetts Medical School and Brigham and Women's Hospital in Boston looked at baseball records from 1991 to 1994. They studied the performance of 19 teams from the Eastern and Pacific time zones, looking at the results of the two games immediately after a team traveled from one coast to the other. The study shows that changing time zones may hurt the performance of West Coast baseball teams traveling east for a game, but not East Coast teams traveling west. The reason, the researchers think, is that people traveling east suffer more from the symptoms of jet lag.

An example of this effect can be seen in the best-of-seven league championship series played in 1993 between the San Francisco Giants and the Atlanta Braves. The winner of the best-of-seven series goes on to play in the World Series to determine the best team in baseball. The games are played in the home cities of each team, so in 1993 the Atlanta Braves and the San Francisco Giants played the first two games in Atlanta, the next three games in San Francisco, and the last two games in Atlanta. In this contest, Atlanta won four of the seven games and was the winner of the series. Researchers believe that the San Francisco Giants lost because they played more games away from home and therefore had more jet lag.

We know from past studies that the symptoms of jet lag are stronger when a person travels east. This is because when we travel east, our day becomes shorter, and a shorter day is more difficult to adjust to than a longer day. So the players from San Francisco were at a disadvantage when they traveled east for a game in Atlanta. The researchers think that the San Francisco team had more of the symptoms caused by jet lag—problems such as headaches, tiredness, and difficulty thinking clearly. All of these symptoms could result in poor performance by baseball players, making the difference between winning and losing a game.

However, this is only the first study to look at the effect of jet lag on sports, and more research is needed. Other scientists say that this research doesn't prove that jet lag causes poor performance in baseball games. This study only looked at baseball records for three years, and much more information must be studied before we can decide if the losses are truly a result of jet lag and not some other reason.

Nevertheless, perhaps some baseball fans on the West Coast won't feel so bad if their team loses this year. Back to you, Kate.

Kate: What about the "home team advantage." Isn't the team that travels away from home at a disadvantage as well?

Jim: Yes, the positive effects of the "home team advantage" are well known in all sports. It's much easier for a team to play a game at home where they can sleep in their own beds and where the local fans can come to the game and cheer for the team. However, jet lag adds to the disadvantage for the team that's playing away from home. So when the San Francisco team traveled east to play in Atlanta, they were at a disadvantage in two ways: They were playing away from home *and* they had strong jet lag from traveling east.

Kate: OK. Thanks Jim. Join us for our health report tomorrow night, when Jim will talk about ways to prevent jet lag when you travel.

C. *Listening for Details*

(repeat Section 3B)

D. *Listening between the Lines*

EXCERPT 1

In the study, doctors from the University of Massachusetts Medical School and Brigham and Women's Hospital in

Boston looked at baseball records from 1991 to 1994. They studied the performance of 19 teams from the Eastern and Pacific time zones, looking at the results of the two games immediately after a team traveled from one coast to the other. The study shows that changing time zones may hurt the performance of West Coast baseball teams traveling east for a game, but not East Coast teams traveling west. The reason, the researchers think, is that people traveling east suffer more from the symptoms of jet lag.

EXCERPT 2

An example of this effect can be seen in the best-of-seven league championship series played in 1993 between the San Francisco Giants and the Atlanta Braves. The winner of the best-of-seven series goes on to play in the World Series to determine the best team in baseball. The games are played in the home cities of each team, so in 1993 the Braves and the Giants played the first two games in Atlanta, the next three games in San Francisco, and the last two games in Atlanta. In this contest, Atlanta won four of the seven games, and was the winner of the series.

EXCERPT 3

We know from past studies that the symptoms of jet lag are stronger when a person travels east. This is because when we travel east, our day becomes shorter, and a shorter day is more difficult to adjust to than a longer day.

EXCERPT 4

The researchers think that the San Francisco team had more of the symptoms caused by jet lag—problems such as headaches, tiredness, and difficulty thinking clearly. All of these symptoms could result in poor performance by baseball players, making the difference between winning and losing a game.

EXCERPT 5

Yes, the positive effects of the "home team advantage" are well known in all sports. It's much easier for a team to play a game at home where they can sleep in their own beds and where the local fans can come to the game and cheer for the team.

4. LISTENING TWO: Jet Lag in the Office

A. *Expanding the Topic*

John: Hi, Muna. Nice to see you back in the office today. How was your trip?

Muna: The trip was fine, but I feel awful. I think it's the jet lag. I can't seem to concentrate on my work. I keep forgetting things, and I feel like my mind is working very slowly. I even had trouble adding some simple numbers! Look, there's Jack. He doesn't look so good either. Is the jet lag getting to you, Jack?

Jack: Is it ever! I keep yawning all the time, and I've been feeling really tired all day. I can't keep my eyes open. I need a big cup of coffee. I think I'll have one of those donuts too. Maybe that will keep me awake!

Rosemary: Hi, everyone.

John: Hi, Rosemary. Welcome back. Would you like a donut?

Rosemary: Oh, no thanks. I don't feel like eating anything. I tried to eat breakfast today, but I just felt sick. It feels like everything I ate yesterday is still in my stomach. I think I'll just have some hot tea.

John: Hi, Marco. Hi, Sarah. Everyone has just been complaining about their jet lag. Has it hit you yet, Marco?

Marco: Oh, yeah. My body is still in the old time zone. Last night, I was tossing and turning. I tried to read, but that didn't make me sleepy. Then I watched TV, but that didn't help either. I finally fell asleep when the sun came up!

John: How about you Sarah?

Sarah: I guess it's the jet lag. I feel awful. My head has been pounding all morning. I took some aspirin, but it didn't help much. My eyes hurt so much it's difficult for me to look at my computer!

John: Wow! You're all feeling so terrible—I don't think you're going to get much work done today. Maybe the boss will let you all go home and recover.

Rosemary: Wouldn't that be nice?

5. REVIEWING LANGUAGE

A. *Exploring Language: Syllable Stress*

EXAMPLE

baseball   adjust   performance

❶

ad/van/tage	hos/pi/tal	se/ries
dif/fi/cult	mea/sure	short/er
dis/ad/van/tage	play/er	symp/tom
doc/tor	prob/lem	tired/ness
ef/fect	rec/ords	trou/ble
head/aches	re/sear/cher	

❷ (repeat Section 5A)

UNIT 3 ◆ TOO GOOD TO BE TRUE

3. LISTENING ONE: Too Good to be True

A. *Introducing the Topic*

Announcer: You're sitting down to dinner, and the phone rings. The man on the phone tells you that you have just won a new car, ten thousand dollars, or a luxury vacation. It sounds wonderful, but can you trust this person on the phone? Our consumer reporter, Nadine Chow, tells us the truth about telephone fraud.

Reporter: Every day, innocent people are victims, losing money to telephone con artists who will tell you anything to get your money. In the United States, people lose about 40 billion dollars each year to telephone fraud. Today, we're going to listen to a real telephone call to learn what these con artists say to get your money, and what you can do to protect yourself.

Frank: Good afternoon, is Ms. Suzanne Markham in?

Suzanne: This is she.

Frank: Suzanne, this is Frank Richland from Western Advertising Incorporated. How are you doing?

Suzanne: I'm fine. How can I help you?

Frank: Ma'am, are you ready for a big surprise?

B. *Listening for Main Ideas*

Announcer: You're sitting down to dinner, and the phone rings. The man on the phone tells you that you have just won a new car, ten thousand dollars, or a luxury vacation. It sounds wonderful, but can you trust this person on the phone? Our consumer reporter, Nadine Chow, tells us the truth about telephone fraud.

Reporter: Every day, innocent people are victims, losing money to telephone con artists who will tell you anything to get your money. In the United States, people lose about 40 billion dollars each year to telephone fraud. Today, we're going to listen to a real telephone call to learn what these con artists say to get your money and what you can do to protect yourself.

Frank: Good afternoon, is Ms. Suzanne Markham in?

Suzanne: This is she.

Frank: Suzanne, this is Frank Richland from Western Advertising Incorporated. How are you doing?

Suzanne: I'm fine. How can I help you?

Frank: Ma'am, are you ready for a big surprise? Because I have some great news! It's my pleasure to tell you that just won our Grand Prize!

Suzanne: The Grand Prize? Really? What do I win?

Frank: You've done it! You have won a luxury car, ten thousand dollars cash, or five thousand dollars cash. You, the lucky winner, will get to choose one of these wonderful prizes! Congratulations!

Suzanne: Oh, my gosh! I don't believe it! Really? I can't believe it!

Reporter: It sounds great, doesn't it? Almost too good to be true. Frank Richland is a telephone con artist. He is using one of the most common frauds—telling the victim she has just won a big prize. The problem is, there aren't any prizes. There's no car; there's no money. However, to make the prize seem real, the con artist talks about what will happen after Suzanne wins the prize.

Frank: The first thing I'm going to need after you've won the prize is to put you on TV, to show you winning the prize—standing by the car or holding the check for ten thousand dollars.

Suzanne: Oh, wow! This is great! When do I find out which prize I get?

Reporter: The con artist has done the first half of his job. Suzanne is excited about winning the prize. But now the con artist tells her what she has to do to get it.

Frank: To receive this prize, you must be a customer of our company, which means you have to have bought something from us within the past year. So, to receive this prize, you need to send a small deposit. Then we will choose the prize and send it to you.

Suzanne: What do I have to do?

Frank: The amount of the deposit I need is five hundred dollars.

Suzanne: That's a lot of money. . . . I'm not sure I have $500 dollars to send you.

Reporter: Now that the victim knows that she has to send money to get the prize, she's not sure if she can trust Frank. To get the money, the con artist has to get the victim's trust.

Frank: Suzanne, it's my job to help you get your prize, just remember that. I can understand that $500 dollars seems like a lot of money. But just remember, in return you will get either the car, ten thousand dollars or five thousand dollars. I know that you would really like to have one of the prizes, and I'd hate to see them go to someone else. You know, in just these few minutes we've been talking, I can tell that you're a special person, and I think you deserve to get this money.

Suzanne: That's so sweet of you. The prize does sound wonderful!

Reporter: After he feels that the victim trusts him, the con artist puts pressure on the victim to make a quick decision, before she has a chance to think about what she's doing.

Frank: So, to make sure I understand, you're sending me five hundred dollars today, so I can send you your prize, right? You must send it now, or else I'll have to give the prize to someone else!

Suzanne: Er . . . OK . . . Who do I send the money to?

Frank: That's Western Advertising Incorporated. Box 703, Western Avenue. . . .

Reporter: What Frank Richland didn't know was that the police were secretly recording the conversation. In our studio today, we have Suzanne Markham to tell us what happened after this call. Suzanne, what happened after you sent in the check for five hundred dollars?

Suzanne: Nothing. I never heard from Western Advertising again.

Reporter: So you didn't receive the car or the money.

Suzanne: That's correct.

Reporter: Did you try to get your money back?

Suzanne: Yes, I did. But when I called the number, the phone had been cut off. The company—Western Advertising Incorporated—was closed.

Reporter: But the question I think everyone wants to know is why did you trust this man? Why did you trust a stranger who called your house and asked you to send so much money?

Suzanne: Well, for one thing, the whole phone call was very exciting, and Frank seemed so nice at the time. So I never really thought that it might be fraud. I guess I'm pretty gullible. I trust people very easily.

Reporter: So what's your advice to people who get these types of phone calls? How can people protect themselves?

Suzanne: Be very careful. Don't agree to send money to someone who calls your house offering a prize. Remember that if something seems too good to be true, it probably is.

Reporter: Thank you, Suzanne. That's wise advice. Back to you, Charlie.

C. *Listening for Details*

(repeat Section 3B)

D. *Listening between the Lines*

1 Excerpt 1

> **Frank:** Ma'am, are you ready for a big surprise? Because I have some great news! It's my pleasure to tell you that you just won our Grand Prize!

Suzanne: The Grand Prize? Really? What do I win?

EXCERPT 2

Frank: The first thing I'm going to need after you've won the prize is to put you on TV, to show you winning the prize—standing by the car or holding the check for ten thousand dollars.

Suzanne: Oh, wow! This is great! When do I find out which prize I get?

EXCERPT 3

Frank: To receive this prize, you must be a customer of our company, which means you have to have bought something from us within the past year. So, to receive this prize, you need to send a small deposit. Then we will choose the prize and send it to you.

Suzanne: What do I have to do?

EXCERPT 4

Frank: I know that you would really like to have one of the prizes, and I'd hate to see them go to someone else. You know, in just these few minutes we've been talking, I can tell that you're a special person, and I think you deserve to get this money.

Suzanne: That's so sweet of you. The prize does sound wonderful!

EXCERPT 5

Frank: So, to make sure I understand, you're sending me five hundred dollars today, so I can send you your prize, right? You must send it now, or else I'll have to give the prize to someone else!

Suzanne: Er . . . OK . . . Who do I send the money to?

2 (repeat Section 3D)

4. LISTENING TWO: Other Victims

A. *Expanding the Topic*

1. **Joe Lau:** I don't really know why I sent him the money. My daughter's always telling me not to give out my credit card number over the phone, but this Frank guy was so nice and so friendly that I believed him. I guess I'm pretty gullible. If someone tells me something I usually believe them. That's OK most of the time, but sometimes it gets me into trouble.

2. **Rosa Alvitas:** Frank seemed like such a nice young man, and so concerned about me. You see, I lost my husband a year ago, and I don't have many friends. I don't get many phone calls and I sometimes get very lonely, so I really enjoyed talking to him. I really thought I could trust him.

3. **Peter Alam:** I've heard about telephone fraud like this, and I always thought I was very careful. But while I was talking to Frank, I kept thinking about the money. I lost my job recently, so I really need some extra money right now. I guess I got very excited about the money he said I'd won, and I just didn't think carefully.

4. **Beth Goldberg:** Well, Frank put so much pressure on me! He kept saying that he wanted to help me, and how I had to decide right away. He said that if I didn't send the money, he would give the prize to someone else. I wasn't

sure I could trust him, but he made me decide so quickly; I just didn't have time to think!

5. REVIEWING LANGUAGE

A. *Exploring Language: Reductions*

1
Student A: Do you <u>wanna</u> get a prize?
Do you <u>wanna</u> get a prize?

Student B: Yes, I <u>wanna</u> get a prize.
Yes, I <u>wanna</u> get a prize.

Student A: First you <u>hafta</u> send the money.
First you <u>hafta</u> send the money.

Student B: I don't <u>wanna</u> send the money.
I don't <u>wanna</u> send the money.

Student A: You <u>hafta</u> send it now.
You <u>hafta</u> send it now.

Student B: I'm <u>gonna</u> call the cops.
I'm <u>gonna</u> call the cops.

UNIT 4 ◆ IF YOU CAN'T BEAT 'EM, JOIN 'EM

3. LISTENING ONE: "If You Can't Beat 'Em, Join 'Em"

A. *Introducing the Topic*

Solomon: . . . You see, they can survive terrible persecution from humans—we give them poison and try to kill them, but they still survive and live happily, so they must be fairly smart. So I thought it would be interesting to breed them. Then perhaps I could train them to do different things.

B. *Listening for Main Ideas*

Reporter: If you have ever had problems with insects in your home, you know how frustrating it can be. You try poison and traps and exterminators, but nothing seems to work. It seems like it's impossible to get rid of those insects. Well, maybe the problem is that you're trying to solve the problem in the wrong way. I talked to entomologist Richard Solomon, a scientist who studies insects, about an experience he had with cockroaches.

Dr. Solomon, tell me the story about you and the cockroaches. What happened exactly?

Solomon: Well, I was living in New York—I think it was 19 . . . 1957—in a terrible neighborhood. It was a sixth-floor apartment, and its great advantage was that the rent was low. That was important because I was a college student at the time. But one of the disadvantages was that there were cockroaches everywhere. So I tried different ways to get rid of them.

Reporter: How did you try to get rid of them?

Solomon: I tried some different things, and ah . . .

Reporter: Did you try poisons and things like that?

Solomon: Well, I didn't want to use poisons 'cause I lived there, and I didn't want the roaches running around, carrying all this poison into my food. I didn't want to do that too much. I tried some things like roach traps and fly swatters, but they didn't really work.

Reporter: What else did you try?

Solomon: Ah, after a while I decided that if I couldn't beat 'em, I'd join 'em. And find a way to . . . uh breed them.

Reporter: Breed them! That's a strange idea. Why did you want to breed them?

Solomon: Well, I felt that as insects go, roaches are fairly smart. You see, they can survive terrible persecution from humans —we give them poison and try to kill them, but they still survive and live happily, so they must be fairly smart. So I thought it would be interesting to breed them. Then perhaps I could train them to do different things.

Reporter: How did you want to train the cockroaches?

Solomon: Well ummm . . . maybe to remember things, for instance, to remember where food was. Or to race . . . to see which cockroach could run faster. But I was more interested in intellectual tasks like remembering.

Reporter: So how did you get ready for this experiment?

Solomon: Well, the first step was to breed the cockroaches and get them to grow. So I collected a whole bunch of them. . . .

Reporter: How did you collect them?

Solomon: They were pretty easy to collect. They were running all over, so I just picked them up and put them in a big jar so they couldn't get away.

Reporter: What did you do next?

Solomon: Well, the question was, what to feed them? I wanted to feed them all the same diet, so that if my experiment worked, I'd know the best diet for roaches. So I tried sugar, because I thought it would give them energy. And I tried fruit, and they seemed to like that. I also gave them some cat food. And they seemed to do OK on that for a while.

Reporter: So your experiment was going well!

Solomon: No, not really, because the cockroaches never laid more eggs, so I never got more than one generation. So in the end, some of the cockroaches lived, but most of them died, and none of them laid any eggs.

Reporter: Did you try to train any of the cockroaches?

Solomon: Not really, because I was busy trying to breed them and figure out what kind of food they liked. And then they all started to die in the jar.

Reporter: What was the result of your experiment?

Solomon: Well, since I only got one generation of cockroaches, in the end I felt the whole thing had been a kind of failure.

Reporter: Did you learn anything?

Solomon: One thing I learned from the experience was that experiments with insects are a lot more difficult than the experiments I usually did, which were electronic experiments. Insects are very unpredictable—you never know what they're going to do! But another thing I learned was that I was very interested in studying insects. I was majoring in electrical engineering, but I changed my major to biology, and eventually I got my Ph.D. in entomology, the biology of insects.

Reporter: Hmm. That's interesting. One more question about the cockroaches. The cockroaches you tried to breed in the jar—they all died. What happened to the roaches in your apartment? Did you ever get rid of them?

Solomon: No . . . no, I didn't.

Reporter: So we can say that if you want to get rid of cockroaches, you should try to breed them, and then they will all die.

Solomon: Yes, I guess you can say that.

Reporter: How do you feel about roaches now? Do you like having cockroaches in your house any better now?

Solomon: No, I don't! I think they are very interesting to study, but I don't like to have them in my house. And I think that the only successful way to get rid of them is to move . . . to another apartment!

C. *Listening for Details*

(repeat Section 3B)

D. *Listening between the Lines*

EXCERPT 1

Solomon: . . . But one of the disadvantages was that there were cockroaches everywhere. So I tried different ways to get rid of them.

Reporter: How did you try to get rid of them?

Solomon: I tried some different things, and ah . . .

Reporter: Did you try poisons and things like that?

Solomon: Well, I didn't want to use poisons 'cause I lived there, and I didn't want the roaches running around carrying all this poison into my food. I didn't want to do that too much. I tried some things like roach traps and fly paper, but they didn't really work.

Reporter: What else did you try?

Solomon: Ah, after a while I decided that if I couldn't beat 'em, I'd join 'em. And find a way to . . . uh breed them.

EXCERPT 2

Reporter: Breed them! That's a strange idea. Why did you want to breed them?

Solomon: Well, I felt that as insects go, roaches are fairly smart. You see, they can survive terrible persecution from humans—we give them poison and try to kill them, but they still survive and live happily, so they must be fairly smart. So I thought it would be interesting to breed them. Then perhaps I could train them to do different things.

Reporter: How did you want to train the cockroaches?

Solomon: Well ummm . . . maybe to remember things, for instance, to remember where food was. Or to race . . . to see which cockroach could run faster. But I was more interested in intellectual tasks like remembering.

EXCERPT 3

Reporter: What was the result of your experiment?

Solomon: Well, since I only got one generation of cockroaches, in the end I felt the whole thing had been a kind of failure.

Reporter: Did you learn anything?

Solomon: One thing I learned from the experience was that experiments with insects are a lot more difficult than the experiments I usually did, which were electronic experiments. Insects are very unpredictable—you never know what they're going to do! (laughter) But another thing I learned was that I was very interested in studying insects. I was majoring in electrical engineering, but I changed my major to biology, and eventually I got my Ph.D. in entomology, the biology of insects.

4. LISTENING TWO: Useful Insects

A. *Expanding the Topic*

❶ **Reporter:** Most people do not like insects very much. We do everything we can to get rid of insects in our house and garden. But actually, some insects are very useful to people. Today, insects are being used in many surprising ways.

For example, insects are very useful in medicine. Believe it or not, maggots are now used regularly in hospitals. When a person gets a very bad injury on their body, the dead skin must be removed. Today, doctors are using maggots to eat the dead skin around the injury. The doctors have found that maggots eat only the dead skin, so they make the injury very clean. Many hospitals keep a supply of maggots for this purpose.

Another useful insect is the mosquito. Often people need medicine, but they live very far away from a doctor. To solve this problem, doctors give the medicine to mosquitoes. The mosquitoes then fly far away, bite people, and give them the medicine.

In the world of medicine and science, fireflies are also useful. Fireflies have a special chemical inside them that makes their bodies shine like fire at night. This chemical can be removed from a firefly's body and used for medical tests. Scientists who do genetic engineering also use this chemical in their experiments.

Another insect that is useful to humans is the termite. In many countries, poor people don't get enough protein to eat. To solve this problem, scientists have used termites to make a protein powder that can be added to food. The termites have a lot of protein, and they are not expensive. This way, many people can receive protein powder that doesn't cost very much.

❷ (repeat Section 4A)

5. REVIEWING LANGUAGE

A. *Exploring Language: Plural* S

❶ ants

butterflies

crickets

cockroaches

fireflies

praying mantises

bees

ladybugs

maggots

mosquitoes

spiders

termites

❷ (repeat Section 5A)

UNIT 5 ◆ UNDERSTANDING ACCENTS

3. LISTENING ONE: Understanding Accents

A. *Introducing the Topic*

Johnson: Come in!

Fredrick: Hi, Professor Johnson! Do you have a minute?

Johnson: Fredrick! Come in.

Fredrick: I like your new office!

Johnson: Thanks! It's much nicer than my old one. . . . What can I do for you?

Fredrick: Well . . . er . . . I'd like to talk about my English.

Johnson: Your English is great! You were my top student last semester. How's your new listening/speaking class with . . . um . . . Professor Simmons, right?

Fredrick: Yeah, Professor Simmons. He's a good teacher . . . but . . . er . . . I'm worried about my classmates.

B. *Listening for Main Ideas*

Johnson: Come in!

Fredrick: Hi, Professor Johnson! Do you have a minute?

Johnson: Fredrick! Come in.

Fredrick: I like your new office!

Johnson: Thanks! It's much nicer than my old one. . . . What can I do for you?

Fredrick: Well . . . er . . . I'd like to talk about my English.

Johnson: Your English is great! You were my top student last semester. How's your new listening/speaking class with . . . um . . . Professor Simmons, right?

Fredrick: Yeah, Professor Simmons. He's a good teacher . . . but . . . er . . . I'm worried about my classmates.

Johnson: Your classmates?

Fredrick: I mean . . . my classmates are from all different countries. I'm afraid that if I talk with them during group work, I'll pick up their accents.

Johnson: I wouldn't worry about that if I were you. There's no way you can pick up a different accent just from being in class a few hours a week.

Fredrick: Really?

Johnson: Really! Just think of all the English you're exposed to every day here in the United States. You listen to the radio, you watch TV, you talk with your American friends, you chat with people in stores. . . . Most of the English you hear is American English. You're only with your classmates a couple of hours a day. That's not going to affect your accent.

Fredrick: Are you sure?

Johnson: Positive! Let me give you an example. . . . Umm . . . say you have a mother from Germany living in the United States. Let's say she has a child here. Even if the mother speaks English with a German accent, her child will still grow up speaking American English. Why? Because the child's getting language from lots of other places, not just the mother. It's the same for your situation.

Fredrick: I understand your example about the child . . . but I think children learn language differently than adults.

Johnson: Actually you're right. It isn't exactly the same because children CAN actually learn accents. Their minds and bodies are much more flexible than ours, so it's easier for them. For adults who are studying a foreign language, accent is one of the hardest things to improve. In fact, most adults never lose their native accents.

Fredrick: Hmmm. . . . So does that mean I'll never sound like a native speaker.

Johnson: Unfortunately that's probably true.

Fredrick: Hmmm . . . that makes me wonder. . . .

Johnson: About what?

Fredrick: About if I should take that pronunciation class that I signed up for next semester. Since I'll never sound like a native speaker, maybe I don't need the class.

Johnson: I wouldn't look at it that way. In a pronunciation class, there are still important things that you can learn.

Fredrick: Like what, for example?

Johnson: Like things that will make your speech clearer—things such as stress, rhythm, and intonation.

Fredrick: I'm sorry. I don't know what these are.

Johnson: Let me give you an example. . . . Umm . . . OK. . . . Today, when I was calling on students in my speaking class, I noticed that one of my students was absent. I asked the class why Sylvia hadn't shown up, . . . and one student said, "Professor, I talked to her this morning and she is homesick." When I heard the word "homesick," I immediately thought that Sylvia was missing her home country and was too depressed to come to school. So I started asking more questions. . . . Was she sad? Did she want to leave the United states to return home? After a few minutes, I realized that Sylvia was at home sick. She just had a bad cold. The student who was telling me about Sylvia said "homesick" instead of "home sick."

Fredrick: Oh! He said the words with the wrong . . . how do you say it . . . er . . .?

Johnson: The wrong stress. The problem was that the student put the stress on the wrong syllable. Problems like this are things that you study in a pronunciation class. . . . And these are really important because if you get them wrong, there can be big misunderstandings.

Fredrick: Like what happened in your class.

Johnson: Exactly! If you use correct stress when you speak, people will usually be able to understand you, even if you have a different accent. For example, if someone had an Indian accent he might say . . . "She is home sick" . . . or if the person was from England he would say . . . "She is home sick."

Fredrick: Or if the person was from Australia he would say . . .

Johnson: "She is home sick"! Were you able to understand all these different accents?

Fredrick: Yes! I'm surprised!

Johnson: That's because the stress was the same.

Fredrick: But even if I can understand different accents, aren't there some accents that are better than others? I've heard people say that a British accent is better than an American accent.

Johnson: Well, from my point of view—and most language teachers would agree—there's no such thing as a "best" accent. Today, there are so many different kinds of English accents around the world. Saying that one accent is "better" or "worse" than another is like saying that one country or group of people is "better" or "worse" than another one. We can't compare them that way—they're just different.

Fredrick: Hmm. I've never thought about it that way.

Johnson: The most important thing is that everyone understands one another, so that's why pronunciation classes are important.

Fredrick: I guess you're right. . . . Uh oh . . . it's getting late. I have to check out a book from the library before class, so I'd better get going. Thanks for your advice. I'll think over what you said.

Johnson: Good to see you! Have a good semester and drop by any time!

Fredrick: Bye! Thanks again!

C. *Listening for Details*

(repeat Section 3B)

D. *Listening between the Lines*

❶ EXCERPT 1

Fredrick: . . . My classmates are from all different countries. I'm afraid that if I talk with them during group work, I'll pick up their accents.

Johnson: I wouldn't worry about that if I were you. There's no way you can pick up a different accent just from being in class a few hours a week.

Fredrick: Really?

EXCERPT 2

Johnson: . . . Just think of all the English you're exposed to every day here in the United States. You listen to the radio, you watch TV, you talk with your American friends, you chat with people in stores. . . . Most of the English you hear is American English. You're only with your classmates a couple of hours a day.

That's not going to affect your accent.

Fredrick: Are you sure?

EXCERPT 3

Johnson: . . . Say you have a mother from Germany living in the United States. Let's say she has a child here. Even if the mother speaks English with a German accent, her child will still grow up speaking American English. Why? Because the child's getting language from lots of other places, not just her mother. It's the same for your situation.

Fredrick: I understand your example about the child . . . but I think children learn language differently than adults.

EXCERPT 4

Johnson: Well, from my point of view—and most language teachers would agree—there's no such thing as a "best" accent. Today, there are so many different kinds of English accents around the world. Saying that one accent is "better" or "worse" than another is like saying that one country or group of people is "better" or "worse" than another one. We can't compare them that way—they're just different.

Fredrick: Hmm. I've never thought about it that way.

EXCERPT 5

Johnson: "The most important thing is that everyone understands one another, so that's why pronunciation classes are important.

Fredrick: I guess you're right."

4. LISTENING TWO: Accents and Children

A. *Expanding the Topic*

Professor: Children are amazing language learners! They're able to pick up new languages quickly and easily, without any accent. Adults, on the other hand, have to study hard to learn another language, and even then, they usually never lose their native accents. Why? What makes children different?

One explanation has to do with the muscles that control the movement in our mouths. In our mouths, there are hundreds of muscles that control the movements of our tongue, lips, cheeks, and so on. In children, these muscles are still flexible, so it's easier for them to move their mouths into new positions to make new sounds. In adults, the muscles are less flexible, so it's more difficult for them to make sounds that aren't in their native language.

Another explanation has to do with our brains. There are two sides to our brains—the left side and the right side. In adults, each side of our brain helps us to do different things. For example, the left side of our brain helps us to think through problems step by step, whereas the right side helps us remember things we see, hear, and feel. In children, however, the brain isn't yet divided into a left and a right side. Some researchers believe that this helps children to be more flexible language learners. In other words, their brains are more open to the differences in a new language.

5. REVIEWING LANGUAGE

A. *Exploring Language: Question Intonation*

Kimiko: Professor Brown. Do you have a minute?

Professor: Yes. How can I help you? Are you having a problem in class?

Kimiko: Oh no! I enjoy your class, but it only meets three hours a week. How can I get more English?

Professor: Well, you could listen to English news programs on the radio.

Kimiko: That's a good idea!

Professor: You could also watch English-language movies. What kinds of movies do you like?

Kimiko: I like comedies. You're right, I should watch more movies. These are good suggestions for listening. Do you have any suggestions for speaking?

Professor: Could you take a pronunciation class? Professor Price is teaching one this semester. Do you know him?

Kimiko: Yes, I do! When does the class meet?

Professor: I'm not sure. You'd better ask him.

Kimiko: I'll do that right now. Thanks for your advice.

Professor: You're welcome!

UNIT 6 ◆ WORKING WITH AIDS PATIENTS

3. LISTENING ONE: Training a Nurse's Assistant

A. *Introducing the Topic*

Susan: Hi, Nicky. How's it going?

Nicky: Hi, Susan.

Susan: How was your first week on the AIDS ward?

Nicky: OK, I guess. But I never realized how many different things nurse's assistants have to do. There's a lot to learn . . . . (pause)

Susan: There sure is! That's why we're having this meeting today, Nicky. As your advisor, it's my responsibility to help you learn your new job. We've found that sometimes our new assistants have trouble adjusting to the AIDS ward.

Nicky: Actually, I *do* feel worried about being here.

B. *Listening for Main Ideas*

Susan: Hi, Nicky. How's it going?

Nicky: Hi, Susan.

Susan: How was your first week on the AIDS ward?

Nicky: OK, I guess. But I never realized how many different things nurse's assistants have to do. There's a lot to learn . . . . (pause)

Susan: There sure is! That's why we're having this meeting today, Nicky. As your advisor, it's my responsibility to help you learn your new job. We've found that sometimes our new assistants have trouble adjusting to the AIDS ward.

Nicky: Actually, I *do* feel worried about being here.

Susan: That's normal. I felt the same way when I started. What are you nervous about?

Nicky: I know it sounds dumb, but I keep thinking that I might get infected with HIV. I know there isn't a very big risk, but I'm still worried. My friends are worried, too.

Susan: What are your friends saying?

Nicky: Well, some of them don't want to be around me now. I think they're afraid that they'll get HIV somehow. One friend always used to give me rides in her car, but she won't drive me to work now because she's afraid I'll get the virus in her car!

Susan: That's a difficult situation. But it's a good opportunity to teach your friends the facts about HIV and AIDS, so they'll know they're wrong. And if they don't want to learn anything, maybe they aren't good friends. I know I lost a few friends when I started working here.

Nicky: My family's also worried. My mother keeps saying, "You can't be too careful!" She's afraid that I'll get AIDS from a patient. So I try to be very careful. I always wear the protective clothing, you know—the rubber gloves, paper clothing, and plastic glasses. But then something strange happened.

Susan: What happened?

Nicky: I went in to see a patient, to bring him his lunch, and he looked at me and said, "Oh, you're new here, aren't you." Then he was acting very angry at me after that. I think it was because of the clothing!

Susan: Why do you think he was angry?

Nicky: I'm not sure. I was just trying to protect myself.

Susan: I think the important thing to remember when you're working with AIDS patients is that you're working with people—people who are very sick, but who still need to be treated with respect. I remember what my boss told me when I first started working with AIDS patients. He said, "It's important to isolate the AIDS virus, but not the AIDS patient."

Nicky: What do you mean by "not isolate the AIDS patient"?

Susan: Well, just imagine that you're very sick. You're lying in bed in the hospital, worrying that you're going to die. Then, every time someone comes in the room, they're covered from head to toe in protective clothing. How would that make you feel?

Nicky: Terrible! It would make me feel like I was dangerous . . . like no one wanted to be near me.

Susan: Exactly. You would feel very isolated. We don't want our AIDS patients to feel that way. It's important that they feel just like all our other patients.

Nicky: So what should I do?

Susan: Well, you have to think carefully before you go into someone's room. We know that it's impossible to get AIDS from just touching someone, or breathing the air next to them, or even sharing a glass of water. AIDS, as you know, is passed though blood or bodily fluids. So when you go into a patient's room, think to yourself: "What am I going to do in here? Will I be in contact with blood or other bodily fluids?" For example, when you serve lunch to someone, do you think you need to wear protective clothing? Is there going to be any blood then?

Nicky: Um, no, I guess not. I guess I don't need to wear the clothing when I serve food.

Susan: How about when you draw someone's blood? Do you need the protective clothing then?

Nicky: Well, there's a chance that I could prick my finger on the needle.

Susan: Right. In that case I'd wear gloves, just to be safe. I guess the rule to live by is to protect yourself when you need to, but don't wear the clothing unnecessarily. Part of our job is to take care of the patients' feelings—as well as their illness—and too much protective clothing can make them feel uncomfortable.

Nicky: You have such a good attitude. Don't you ever get depressed? You know, working with sick people all the time who will never get better. . . . I'm not sure I can handle it.

Susan: It is sad sometimes, but remember that many people in the AIDS ward do get better. They aren't cured of AIDS, but they can become healthy again and go back to their lives. Especially now, with so many new AIDS medicines, many people live for a long time. But unfortunately, many people do die as well. Sometimes, when you've been working with a patient for a long time, and that person dies, it's almost like losing a good friend. But on the other hand, you'll meet some of the most wonderful people here. There are people who are sick and dying, but they are still trying to be happy and live as best they can.

Nicky: I feel a little bit better now. It's good to talk to someone who has experience.

Susan: I know. It's a difficult job, but I think you'll find it very rewarding in the end. And any time you want to talk, just let me know.

Nicky: Thanks a lot. I really appreciate it!

C. *Listening for Details*

(repeat Section 3B)

D. *Listening between the Lines*

EXCERPT 1

Nicky: One friend always used to give me rides in her car, but she won't drive me to work now because she's afraid I'll get the virus in her car!

Susan: That's a difficult situation. But it's a good opportunity to teach your friends the facts about HIV and AIDS, so they'll know they're wrong. And if they don't want to learn anything, maybe they aren't good friends. I know I lost a few friends when I started working here.

Nicky: My family's also worried. My mother keeps saying, "You can't be too careful!"

EXCERPT 2

Nicky: What do you mean by "not isolate the AIDS patient"?

Susan: Well, just imagine that you're very sick. You're lying in bed in the hospital, worrying that you're going to die. Then, every time someone comes in the room, they're covered from head to toe in protective clothing. How would that make you feel?

Nicky: Terrible! It would make me feel like I was dangerous . . . like no one wanted to be near me.

Susan: Exactly. You would feel very isolated. We don't want our AIDS patients to feel that way. It's important that they feel just like all our other patients.

EXCERPT 3

Susan: . . . When you serve lunch to someone, do you think you need to wear protective clothing? Is there going to be any blood then?

Nicky: Um, no, I guess not. I guess I don't need to wear the clothing when I serve food.

Susan: How about when you draw someone's blood? Do you need the protective clothing then?

Nicky: Well, there's a chance that I could prick my finger on the needle.

Susan: Right. In that case I'd wear gloves, just to be safe. I guess the rule to live by is to protect yourself when you need to but don't wear the clothing unnecessarily. Part of our job is to take care of the patients' feelings—as well as their illness—and too much protective clothing can make them feel uncomfortable.

Nicky: You have such a good attitude.

4. LISTENING TWO: Calling an AIDS Hotline

A. *Expanding the Topic*

CALL 1

Hotline: Hello. AIDS Hotline.

Caller: Hi. I have a question.

Hotline: Yes?

Caller: Last weekend I went camping with some people from work, and I know one of the people has HIV. There were lots of mosquitoes at the campsite, and I got tons of bites. I'm wondering. . . . Could I get AIDS if a mosquito bites a person with HIV and then bites me?

Hotline: Don't worry! You can't get HIV from an insect. If a mosquito bites someone with HIV, the virus dies once it enters the mosquito.

CALL 2

Hotline: Hello. AIDS Hotline.

Caller: Hi. Can I ask you something?

Hotline: Sure!

Caller: I'm wondering if you can get HIV from kissing someone. I . . . er . . . went on a date last night . . . and you know. . . .

Hotline: OK. I get the picture. Kissing is generally fine. The virus can live in your mouth, but the amount is so little, chances are you won't get HIV that way.

CALL 3

Hotline: Hello. AIDS Hotline.

Caller: Hi. I'm wondering about getting HIV from my dentist. I read somewhere about the woman who got AIDS from going to her dentist.

Hotline: It's possible, but unlikely. Do you know how your dentist cleans his tools?

Caller: No, I don't.

Hotline: Well, you should make sure that your dentist uses an autoclave.

Caller: An autoclave?

Hotline: It's a machine that cleans things at high temperatures.

5. REVIEWING LANGUAGE

A. *Exploring Language:* Can/Can't

A: <u>Can</u> a mother give HIV to her baby when she's pregnant?

B: Yes, she <u>can</u>. She <u>can</u> also pass it to her baby in her milk.

A: What if she feeds the baby with a bottle?

B: She <u>can't</u> pass HIV by giving the baby milk in a bottle.

1. You can't go in there without protective clothing.
2. The patient can leave the hospital today.
3. She can work this weekend.
4. Can't you tell me what the problem is?
5. The doctor can't see you now.
6. You can take an HIV test here.
7. You can go in there. Yes, you can.
8. These gloves can protect you.
9. The hospital can treat AIDS patients.
10. He can't understand how he got AIDS.

UNIT 7 ◆ ENGINE TROUBLE

3. LISTENING ONE: Engine Trouble

A. *Introducing the Topic*

Roy: Now, if you want to call us with a question about your car, or anything else for that matter . . . we're not, we're not just talking about automobiles here.

Bob: Absolutely. In fact, we don't know much about cars, but then, we don't know much about anything else either!

Roy: Our number is 1-800-555-CARS. This is Roy.

Bob: And this is Bob. Hello, you're on *Engine Trouble*.

Frank: Hi, this is Frank calling from Colorado.

Roy: Frank!

Bob: How're you doing, man?

Frank: Great, great. I've got a problem, though. Maybe you guys can help me solve . . . a question I have.

B. *Listening for Main Ideas*

Roy: Now, if you want to call us with a question about your car, or anything else for that matter . . . we're not, we're not just talking about automobiles here.

Bob: Absolutely. In fact, we don't know much about cars, but then, we don't know much about anything else either!

Roy: Our number is 1-800-555-CARS. This is Roy.

Bob: And this is Bob. Hello, you're on *Engine Trouble*.

Frank: Hi, this is Frank calling from Colorado.

Roy: Frank!

Bob: How're you doing, man?

Frank: Great, great. I've got a problem, though. Maybe you guys can help me solve . . . a question I have.

Bob & Roy: Sure.

Frank: Unfortunately, I have to carpool with my wife to work. She likes to carpool 'cause she drives in the morning, and I drive home at night—when she's tired. But I don't like to carpool with her because we always have the same argument.

Roy: Uh-huh.

Frank: When it, when it snows out here and the roads get all ice packed and full of snow, we drive together in our four-wheel drive pickup truck, and when we go home at night—

Bob: Wait, let me stop you here. Frank, do you live in the country?

Frank: Uh, no. I live in the suburbs, and I work in the city.

Bob: And you have a pickup truck with four-wheel drive?

Frank: Yeah, and when we drive home at night. . . .

Bob: Why?

Frank: Huh?

Roy: Oh, come on, Bob. Let the guy ask his question. . . .

Bob: No, why do you have a pickup truck with four-wheel drive in the suburbs? It's so big, and it gets terrible gas mileage.

Frank: I know, but actually, it's useful sometimes to carry things, and when there's a lot of snow. . . .

Bob: But don't you think a sedan or a station wagon is a better car in the suburbs?

Frank: And also my wife likes it. She thinks it's cool. . . .

Bob: Ah-hah! Now we're getting somewhere! Your wife thinks it's cool. . .

Roy: Frank, just ignore Bob's rude questions here. Let's get back to your question.

Bob: Well, excuse me.

Frank: Um, OK. . . . Well, when we drive home at night, I don't use four-wheel drive, because I get terrible gas mileage, probably five miles to the gallon. And my wife constantly tells me to use four-wheel drive when we go home, because she says the truck brakes better. I keep telling her that I don't need four-wheel drive because the brakes don't have anything to do with four-wheel drive.

Roy: So you don't use four-wheel drive because you don't think it helps the truck brake better.

Frank: Right! But my wife disagrees and then one day I stopped suddenly and I almost hit someone, and we didn't talk for two days because she . . . because I wasn't using four-wheel drive.

Roy: But on the way home at night, the roads aren't usually covered with snow and ice, right? They're dry roads at this point?

Frank: Yeah, they're dry roads. Usually at night, all the snow is gone.

Roy: Because it depends on the roads. If the roads are covered with snow and ice, then four-wheel drive is helpful. But on dry, paved roads, no, you shouldn't use four-wheel drive because you can't steer the car well on dry roads when you're in four-wheel drive.

Frank: Right, so I'm right—I don't need to use four-wheel drive.

Roy: I think so.

Bob: Well, it depends on . . . your relationship with your wife.

Roy: That's . . . well, you're right, an important point.

Bob: Frank! How old are you, Frank, . . . how old?

Frank: Well, I'm 36 and she's 27, so we have all these problems in the car, like what radio station, and whether we're going to stop for coffee, and it goes on and on.

Bob: Well, I have my own rule of marriage, and it is . . . it's more important to be happy than to be right. Now you may know that you're right—I mean, I'm always right. When my wife and I have an argument, I'm always right, *but,* being the clever fellow that I am, I never try to tell her that I'm right. And she thinks that I'm a dummy, 'cause I'm always wrong, but she loves me. See? I would keep my mouth shut if I were you, Frank. Just make your wife happy and use the four-wheel drive.

Frank: But four-wheel drive really cuts down on my gas mileage!

Bob: OK, so here's the answer. This is a perfect win-win situation. You can stop using four-wheel drive *and* make your wife happy. Here's what you do: You can explain to your wife—what's her name?

Frank: Margaret.

Bob: Margaret. You say, "Margaret, you know, I called Bob and Roy at *Engine Trouble,* and you won't believe this, but we're both right about this. Imagine that! They told me it should *not* be in four-wheel drive, but for a different reason."

Frank: OK.

Roy: Aaahh.

Bob: It shouldn't be in four-wheel drive because you can't steer the car well on dry, paved roads. Just tell her that, and say, "You're right, hon. You're right, hon!" Trust me, you say that enough times, and you'll be happy.

Frank: OK.

Roy: Yes, and practice saying this: "Yes, dear."

Bob: "Yes, dear" is good, too.

Roy: Good luck, Frank.

Frank: Thanks a lot.

Bob: They'll be in divorce court in six months.

C. *Listening for Details*

(repeat Section 3B)

D. *Listening between the Lines*

PART 1

Excerpt 1: Frank: Unfortunately, I have to carpool with my wife to work. She likes to carpool 'cause she drives in the morning and I drive home at night—when she's tired. But I don't like to carpool with her because we always have the same argument.

Roy: Uh-huh.

Excerpt 2: Frank: Uh, no. I live in the suburbs, and I work in the city.

Bob: And you have a pickup truck with four-wheel drive?

Frank: Yeah, and when we drive home at night. . . .

Bob: Why?

Frank: Huh?

Excerpt 3: Roy: So you don't use four-wheel drive because you don't think it helps the truck brake better.

Frank: Right! But my wife disagrees. . . .

Excerpt 4: Roy: But on the way home at night, the roads are not usually covered with snow and ice, right? They're dry roads at this point?

Frank: Yeah, they're dry. Usually at night, all the snow is gone.

PART 2

Excerpt 5: Frank: I know, but actually, it's useful sometimes to carry things, and when there's a lot of snow. . . .

Bob: But don't you think a sedan or a station wagon is a better car in the suburbs?

Frank: And also my wife likes it. She thinks it's cool. . . .

Bob: Ah-hah! Now we're getting somewhere! Your wife thinks it's cool. . . .

Excerpt 6: Bob: When my wife and I have an argument, I'm always right, *but,* being the clever fellow that I am, I never try to tell her that I'm right. And she thinks that I'm a dummy, 'cause I'm always wrong, but she loves me. (laughter) See? I would keep my mouth shut if I were you, Frank.

Excerpt 7: Bob: You say, "Margaret, you know, I called Bob and Roy at *Engine Trouble*, and you won't believe this, but we're both right about this. Imagine that! Because, they told me it should *not* be in four-wheel drive, but for a different reason."

Frank: OK.

Roy: Aaahh.

Excerpt 8: Bob: Just tell her that, and say, "You're right, hon. You're right, hon!" Trust me, you say that enough times, and you'll be happy.

Frank: OK.

Roy: Yes, and practice saying this: "Yes, dear."

4. LISTENING TWO: More Engine Trouble

A. *Expanding the Topic*

1. CALL 1

Roy: Hello, you're on *Engine Trouble*.

Caller 1: Hi. I just bought a new sport utility vehicle, but I'm really unhappy with the gas mileage I'm getting.

Roy: You want to cut down on your gas mileage, right?

Caller 1: Right. I'm spending too much money on gas.

Roy: Well, unfortunately, that type of automobile does use a lot of gas. But there are a couple of things you can do.

Caller 1: OK.

CALL 2

Bob: Hello, you're on *Engine Trouble*.

Caller 2: Hi. I have a problem. I'm having an argument with my husband.

Bob: Oh, good! We're good at these marriage questions!

Caller 2: The thing is . . . he has this really old car. I mean, really old. From the 1960s, I think. Anyway, I hate the car. It's noisy, it gets terrible gas mileage, it's uncomfortable—you

name it, in every way it's terrible. I want him to sell the car and get a new one, but he loves his old car. What should I do?

CALL 3

Roy: Hello, you're on *Engine Trouble*.

Caller 3: Hi. I have a question about buying a car. I've never had a car before, and I'm wondering what I should look for. A lot of my friends think I should get a sports car, or a pickup truck, because they think they're cool. I've seen some really nice-looking cars, but I'm not sure.

3. CALL 1

Roy: Hello, you're on *Engine Trouble*.

Caller 1: Hi. I just bought a new sport/utility vehicle, but I'm really unhappy with the gas mileage I'm getting.

Roy: You want to cut down on your gas mileage, right?

Caller 1: Right. I'm spending too much money on gas.

Roy: Well, unfortunately, that type of automobile does use a lot of gas. But there are a couple of things you can do.

Caller 1: OK.

Roy: For one thing, don't drive too fast because going fast uses more gas. Also try not to go fast and then stop suddenly.

Bob: But you know the best way to cut down on your gas mileage?

Caller 1: What's that?

Bob: Take the bus!

CALL 2

Bob: Hello, you're on *Engine Trouble*.

Caller 2: Hi. I have a problem. I'm having an argument with my husband.

Bob: Oh, good! We're good at these marriage questions!

Caller 2: The thing is . . . he has this really old car. I mean, really old. From the 1960s, I think. Anyway, I hate the car. It's noisy, it gets terrible gas mileage, it's uncomfortable—you name it, in every way it's terrible. I want him to sell the car and get a new one, but he loves his old car. What should I do?

Roy: Hmmm. Well, I think this is an argument that you will never win. I think he's never going to sell his car. You just have to live with it.

Bob: But if you're really unhappy, just spend the extra money and get a new car for yourself, and maybe when he sees how nice it is, he'll change his mind.

Caller 2: Well, OK, maybe you're right. Thanks!

CALL 3

Roy: Hello, you're on *Engine Trouble*.

Caller 3: Hi. I have a question about buying a car. I've never had a car before, and I'm wondering what I should look for. A lot of my friends think I should get a sports car, or a pickup truck, because they think they're cool. I've seen some really nice-looking cars, but I'm not sure.

Bob: Well, that's not the best way to buy a car. You should be more practical.

Roy: Yeah. First, you should decide what kind of car is best for you now and in the future. Are you going to be single for a long time, when a small car is OK? Or do you think you'll have a family in a few years, when a sports car will be too small? You should also think about the gas mileage and the number of repairs the car will need, because gas and repairs can cost a lot of money.

Caller 3: OK, you've given me a lot to think about. Thanks!

5. REVIEWING LANGUAGE

A. *Exploring Language: Intonation*

1 **Mechanic:** What's the problem?

Car Owner: I was driving home last night and suddenly my car stopped for no reason.

Mechanic: I see. But nothing unusual has happened before this, right?

Car Owner: Right. Everything has been normal.

Mechanic: It might be a problem with your engine. I'm going to check that first, OK?

Car Owner: OK. Do you know how long it will take for you to repair the car?

Mechanic: Well, I can start working on it now. It will probably take a day to fix the problem.

Car Owner: So, you think it will be done tomorrow, right?

Mechanic: Right. You can pick it up in the morning, OK?

Car Owner: OK. But please call me if there are any problems.

2 (repeat Section 3D)

UNIT 8 ◆ YOU ARE WHAT YOU WEAR

3. LISTENING ONE: Traditional Dress in Sri Lanka

A. *Introducing the Topic*

Announcer: Today we begin our series on "Traditional Dress throughout the World." Our journey takes us to the little island nation of Sri Lanka. Shanika DeSilva, a native Sri Lankan now living in the United States, shares some interesting thoughts on traditional dress in her home country.

B. *Listening for Main Ideas*

PART 1

Interviewer: Shanika, thanks for speaking with us today.

Shanika: My pleasure.

Interviewer: First of all, I'd like to ask you . . . what is the traditional clothing in Sri Lanka?

Shanika: Well, the traditional clothing for women is a sari.

Interviewer: And what's a sari?

Shanika: It's a long piece of cloth that is wrapped around your waist, and then it goes over your shoulder.

Interviewer: And do most women in Sri Lanka wear saris?

Shanika: Most of the older women, like my grandmother, wear a sari every day, all the time. The younger women tend to wear dresses or pants or something.

Interviewer: Why don't the younger women wear saris?

Shanika: Well, I guess some of them feel that saris are uncomfortable. I've heard women say that saris are hot and difficult to walk in because they're long. Also, if you're not used to wearing a sari, you might feel afraid that it will come unravelled. It's hard to relax in that situation.

Interviewer: Sounds like saris aren't very practical.

Shanika: Some people feel that way. Also, many younger women think saris are old-fashioned. When you're younger, you're more interested in being stylish. Saris are great for formal occasions, like weddings, but if you're going out with your friends, you want to be more modern.

Interviewer: So the younger women want to be more modern.

Shanika: Actually I shouldn't say all the younger women. It depends a lot on your family history. You see there are two main groups of people in Sri Lanka—the Sinhalese and the Tamils. Then there are some other ethnic groups, like the Sri Lankans, who are part European. The women who are part European tend to be more modern. But the women who are Sinhalese or Tamil tend to be more traditional.

Interviewer: Why are the Sinhalese and Tamils more traditional?

Shanika: It's their culture. Well, in the past, the Sri Lankans that were part European had relatives who wore Western clothing, so they were used to Western dress. The Sinhalese and Tamils didn't have that.

Interviewer: So you're saying that previous family history can influence the way you dress.

Shanika: Yes, I think so.

Interviewer: We've been talking about what women wear. How about the men? Do they have special traditional clothing?

Shanika: Umm . . . the men, I guess, used to wear a sarong, which is a long piece of cloth that's wrapped around the waist.

Interviewer: You say they used to wear sarongs. Don't they wear them anymore?

Shanika: People who live in rural areas, in the country, still wear sarongs. But in the city, it's only the politicians who wear them. People who have office jobs in downtown Colombo wear pants and shirts and even ties. They only wear sarongs to relax at home.

Interviewer: Why don't they wear traditional clothes?

Shanika: I think, personally, that it's a result of being colonized. You see . . . Sri Lanka used to be ruled by the British. Let's see. . . . It was from . . . er . . . 1815 to 1948. Since the men were the ones who went to work, they had to adapt to the kind of clothes the British were wearing at work. The women, on the other hand, didn't leave the house, so they hung on to the traditional form of dress.

Interviewer: Interesting! But what about the men who are politicians? You said before that they still wear traditional dress.

Shanika: Yeah. . . . I think that's also a result of colonization. You see, after the British left, people wanted to show that they were proud of their culture and their new independence. To show their pride, a lot of politicians who used to wear a suit to work, started to wear a sarong.

Interviewer: So it sounds as if political changes in Sri Lanka have influenced the way politicians dress.

Shanika: That's right.

Interviewer: Very interesting! I'm sorry but we have to stop for a break. (to the audience) We'll be back with Part 2 of this discussion in a minute.

PART 2

Interviewer: In case you've just started listening, I'm talking with Shanika De Silva about traditional clothing in Sri Lanka. Shanika, can I switch gears a little and ask you kind of a personal question?

Shanika: Sure!

Interviewer: I'm wondering how you feel about traditional clothing for your children. If you had children, would you want them to wear traditional clothing at certain times, or does it not matter to you?

Shanika: Ummm. . . . I think if I had a daughter it would be fun for her to have at least one sari. I think I would try to teach her to have some pride in her culture and let her know that this is what you would wear.

Interviewer: Why a daughter and not a son?

Shanika: Well, I guess it's because when I was growing up it was the women who wore traditional dress, not the men.

Interviewer: And how about you? Is it important for you to have traditional clothing?

Shanika: It's funny, because when I was a kid growing up in Sri Lanka I didn't think I would ever want to wear saris. But now that I'm older, I like to wear them sometimes. Like my wedding . . . I wore a white sari with gold thread for my wedding.

Interviewer: Why has your attitude changed do you think?

Shanika: Ummm . . . I guess when you get older you see the value in it more. When you're younger, you're more interested in being hip . . . you know . . . wearing Levi's and stuff like that. Now I think about saris as something unique . . . something unusual from my culture. It's nice to have something different to wear, and in the U.S. a sari is really exotic!

Interviewer: It certainly is! Well, this has been very interesting. Unfortunately, that's all we have time for today. Thanks for talking with us.

Shanika: You're welcome!

C. *Listening for Details*

(repeat Section 3B)

D. *Listening between the Lines*

EXCERPT 1

Interviewer: Why don't the younger women wear saris?

Shanika: Well, I guess some of them feel that saris are uncomfortable. I've heard women say that saris are hot and difficult to walk in because they're long. Also, if you're not used to wearing a sari, you might feel afraid that it will come unraveled. It's hard to relax in that situation.

EXCERPT 2

Interviewer: Sounds like saris aren't very practical.

Shanika: Some people feel that way. Also, many younger women think saris are old-fashioned. When you're younger, you're more interested in being stylish. Saris are great for formal occasions, like weddings, but if you're going out with your friends you want to be more modern.

EXCERPT 3

Interviewer: Interesting! But what about the men who are politicians? You said before that they still wear traditional dress.

Shanika: Yeah. . . . I think that's also a result of colonization. You see, after the British left, people wanted to show that they were proud of their culture and their new independence. To show their pride, a lot of politicians who used to wear a suit to work, started to wear a sarong.

EXCERPT 4

Interviewer: And how about you? Is it important for you to have traditional clothing?

Shanika: It's funny, because when I was a kid growing up in Sri Lanka I didn't think I would ever want to wear saris. But now that I'm older, I like to wear them sometimes. Like my wedding . . . I wore a white sari with gold thread for my wedding.

EXCERPT 5

Interviewer: Why has your attitude changed do you think?

Shanika: Ummm . . . I guess when you get older you see the value in it more. When you're younger, you're more interested in being hip . . . you know . . . wearing Levi's and stuff like that. Now I think about saris as something unique . . . something unusual from my culture. It's nice to have something different to wear, and in the U.S. a sari is really exotic!

4. LISTENING TWO: Traditional Dress in Kuwait

A. *Expanding the Topic*

Interviewer: Abdullah, thanks for speaking with us today.

Abdullah: You're welcome.

Interviewer: Could you describe the traditional clothing in your country?

Abdullah: Well, the men wear a *dishdasha*. It's like a long shirt with long sleeves. For the summer we wear white ones, and for winter we have other colors, like brown and so on. And on our heads we wear a *quitra*, which is a piece of cloth, and an *igal*, which is a piece of rope that you put around your head to keep the quitra on.

Interviewer: And do men wear traditional clothes a lot?

Abdullah: Yes. I'd say most of the men do.

Interviewer: For both formal and informal occasions?

Abdullah: Sure. It's a way for us to show pride in our culture.

Interviewer: How about the women? What do they wear?

Abdullah: Most women don't have traditional clothing anymore.

Interviewer: Oh really?

Abdullah: They used to wear something like a big, black coat to cover themselves. It's called an *abaya*, and it covers you completely, but now that's disappearing.

Interviewer: So what do women wear now?

Abdullah: Oh, jeans and dresses and things like that. Only the most traditional women wear the abaya.

Interviewer: Really! Hmmm. . . . We've been talking about wearing traditional clothes in Kuwait. How about in the U.S.? Do you ever wear a dishdasha in the U.S.?

Abdullah: Not really. Maybe once in a while if there's a special holiday at my family's house, but just to go out with my American friends . . . no.

Interviewer: Why not?

Abdullah: I guess it feels strange. If I wear it I feel like everyone's looking at me . . . like I'm some kind of exotic animal or something. I prefer to wear jeans with my American friends. It's more comfortable for me.

5. REVIEWING LANGUAGE

A. *Exploring Language: Thought Groups*

1. Most of the older women, like my grandmother, wear a sari every day.
2. Saris are great for formal occasions, but if you're going out with your friends you want to be more modern.
3. Previous family history can influence the way you dress.
4. The men used to wear a sarong, which is a long piece of cloth that's wrapped around the waist.
5. People who have office jobs wear pants and shirts and even ties.
6. A dishdasha is like a long shirt with long sleeves.
7. For the summer we wear white ones and for the winter we have other colors.
8. On our heads we wear a quitra, which is a piece of cloth, and an igal, which is a piece of rope.
9. It's called an abaya, and it covers you completely.
10. If I wear it, I feel like everyone's looking at me.

UNIT 9 ◆ TO SPANK OR NOT TO SPANK?

3. LISTENING ONE: A Radio Report

A: *Introducing the Topic*

Reporter: Surveys have shown that most parents in the United States—about two-thirds—agree that spanking is an acceptable form of discipline, although that number has been declining in recent years. And although many parents don't think spanking is the best way to discipline children, most parents admit to having hit their children at least once. But even doctors disagree about the issue of corporal punishment.

B. *Listening for Main Ideas*

Announcer: A father was recently arrested by the police for spanking his child, starting a debate among the American public about spanking. Is spanking, or other types of corporal punishment, an acceptable form of discipline for children? Or is it a form of child abuse? Charles Dean has our report.

Reporter: The case that has everyone talking is the arrest of Dale Clover, a thirty-six-year-old father of three, at a shopping mall in St. Louis, Missouri. He was arrested after an employee at the mall saw him spanking his five-year-old son Donny and called the police. Clover was arrested for child abuse. Mr. Clover admits that he hit his son but says that it wasn't child abuse. "Spanking is the only thing that keeps Donny out of trouble," says Clover. "It's not child abuse. It's discipline." Across the country, parents disagree on this issue: What is the difference between loving discipline and child abuse?

Parent 1: A little bit of pain is necessary to teach a child what is right and wrong. It's like burning your hand when you touch a hot stove. Pain is nature's way of teaching us.

Reporter: Some parents, like Rhonda Moore, see a clear difference between spanking and child abuse.

Parent 1: Spanking is done out of love. Child abuse is done out of anger, when the parent loses control. When I spank my children, I always talk to them before and afterwards, and explain why they are being spanked. I explain what they did wrong, and they remember not to do it again. They respect me as a parent. My children understand that I'm spanking them for their own good.

Parent 2: I want my children to learn right and wrong, but not out of fear of being hit. Spanking teaches children to fear their parents, not respect them.

Reporter: Taylor Robinson, father of four, feels that parents should never hit their children for any reason.

Parent 2: When a parent spanks a child, what the child learns is that problems should be solved with violence. They learn that it's acceptable for parents to hurt their children. None of these are lessons that I want to teach my children. I want my children to learn to talk about their problems and solve them without violence, but spanking doesn't teach that.

Reporter: Surveys have shown that a majority of parents in the United States—about two-thirds—agree that spanking is an acceptable form of discipline, although that number has been declining in recent years. And although many parents don't think spanking is the best way to discipline children, most parents admit to having hit their children at least once. Even doctors disagree about the issue of corporal punishment.

Doctor 1: Today, many children don't respect their parents. Children need strong, loving discipline. Sometimes spanking is the best way to get a child's attention, to make sure the child listens to the parent.

Reporter: Dr. John Oparah thinks our child abuse laws sometimes go too far.

Doctor 1: I've know loving parents who have had police officers come to their door and say, "Your child reported that you hit him." They're treated like criminals. As a society, we complain all the time that our young people are getting into more and more trouble, committing crimes—yet when parents try to control their children, they are punished. Some parents are afraid to discipline their children because the children say that they will call the police.

Reporter: However, most doctors say that there are many harmful effects of spanking. Dr. Beverly Lau is opposed to spanking.

Doctor 2: In the long run, spanking doesn't work well; it's not as effective as other forms of discipline. A child may stop misbehaving for the moment, but over time, children who are spanked actually misbehave more than children who are not spanked. From my experience, if you want a peaceful family, don't spank your kids.

Reporter: Spanking causes problems for children as they get older?

Doctor 2: Spanking can lead to more violent behavior in children. Studies show that children who are spanked are more violent than children who are not spanked. They will hit other children more often, and when they grow up they are more likely to hit their own children. These children learn that violence is the best way to respond to problems.

Reporter: It's difficult for some parents to know the difference between spanking and child abuse.

Doctor 2: Supporters of spanking say it's OK to hit my child with my hand, but what about a belt or a stick? Is that OK? Can I leave a bruise? On what part of his body is it OK to hit him? Can I hit him harder if he does something really bad? It's difficult for some parents to know when to stop, especially when they are angry. Eighty-five percent of cases of serious child abuse start when a parent disciplines a child by spanking, but the punishment goes too far and really hurts the child.

Reporter: The issue of spanking and corporal punishment will continue to be debated among parents and in the courts. In Dale Clover's case, he could get up to five years in prison if he is convicted of child abuse.

C. *Listening for Details*

(repeat Section 3B)

D. *Listening between the Lines*

EXCERPT 1

Parent 1: Spanking is done out of love. Child abuse is done out of anger, when the parent loses control. When I spank my children, I always talk to them before and afterwards, and explain why they are being spanked. They respect me as a parent. My children understand that I'm spanking them for their own good.

EXCERPT 2

Parent 2: When a parent spanks a child, what the child learns is that problems should be solved with violence. They learn that it's acceptable for parents to hurt their children. None of these are lessons that I want to teach my children. I want my children to learn to talk about their problems and solve them without violence, but spanking doesn't teach that.

EXCERPT 3

Doctor 1: Today, many children don't respect their parents. Children need strong, loving discipline. Sometimes spanking is the best way to get a child's attention, to make sure the child listens to the parent.

EXCERPT 4

Doctor 2: In the long run, spanking doesn't work well, it's not as effective as other forms of discipline. A child may stop misbehaving for the moment, but over time, children who are spanked actually misbehave more than children who are not spanked. From my experience, if you want a peaceful family, don't spank your kids.

4. LISTENING TWO: Expert Opinions

A. *Expanding the Topic*

Announcer: What are the long-term effects of spanking as a child gets older and becomes an adult? Listen to the opinions of four experts. Donald Sterling, a lawyer and psychologist who interviews criminals before they go to trial. . . .

Sterling: I've seen it over and over again. Violent criminals were almost always were spanked and hit when they were children. This corporal punishment teaches children to be violent when they are very young, so when they are adults, they commit crimes and abuse their wives and children. And then their children grow up to be violent, and the cycle continues.

Announcer: Dr. Phyllis Jones from the Center for Family Research. . . .

Jones: We studied 332 families to see how parents' actions affected teenagers' behavior. We found that teenagers did better when they had clear discipline as a child. Some of these parents used spanking as a means of discipline. It seems that spanking doesn't hurt children if it's done in a loving home, but it's most important to talk to your children and spend time with them. Whether to spank or not should be the choice of the parents.

Announcer: Dr. Armando Mazzone, a back specialist from Somino Medical Center. . . .

Mazzone: Spanking can cause serious health problems. At the hospital, we see children who are injured by spanking. In fact, there are many adults with back problems, and researchers think that some of these back problems could be caused by spankings that they received when they were children.

Announcer: Lois Goldin, child psychologist. . . .

Goldin: In the United States, the number of parents who spank their kids is going down, and people who oppose spanking say that's good because it will make our society less violent. But look at the statistics. Actually, violent crime is rising every year, and the number of teenagers and children that commit crimes is going up the fastest! Parents need to control their children better, and corporal punishment is one way to do that.

UNIT 10 ◆ A MARRIAGE AGREEMENT

3. LISTENING ONE: A Marriage Agreement

A. *Introducing the Topic*

Announcer: This is a marriage agreement between Bob and Jane Parsons. It was written with love and the wish to make each other happy. We both agree not to break the rules outlined in this agreement.

Signed,

Bob: Bob Parsons

Jane: Jane Parsons

Reporter: Bob, Jane, first I'd like to ask you why you decided to write this unusual agreement.

Reporter: So, do you spend a lot of time checking to see if the other person is following the rules? Arguing?

Reporter: What happens if one of you breaks a rule?

Reporter: Do you think other couples should follow your example and write marriage agreements of their own?

B. *Listening for Main Ideas*

Announcer: This is a marriage agreement between Bob and Jane Parsons. It was written with love and the wish to make each other happy. We both agree not to break the rules outlined in this agreement.

Signed,

Bob: Bob Parsons

Jane: Jane Parsons

Reporter: When most couples marry, they may discuss some things in advance, like how many children they want to have or where they want to live, but most of the day-to-day details and problems of married life are worked out after marriage. Not so with the Parsons, who have a fifteen-page marriage agreement that states the rules they must follow in almost every part of their married life.

Announcer: Article 1: Household Chores. Both Bob and Jane will share the household chores. Jane will be responsible for the shopping, cooking, and taking care of the garden. Bob will be responsible for the laundry, cleaning the house, and car repairs.

Reporter: Bob, Jane, first I'd like to ask you why you decided to write this unusual agreement. You've both been married before, am I right?

Bob: Yes. I've been married twice, and Jane was married once before.

Jane: So we have some experience about what goes wrong in a marriage.

Announcer: Article 1a: Grocery Shopping. Jane will do the grocery shopping. She will always use a shopping list at the grocery store.

Bob: Yes, we found that many problems are caused when a person has different expectations than his or her spouse. We wanted to talk about everything openly and honestly before we started living together.

Jane: Also we both know how important it is to respect each other's pet peeves. Like, it used to really annoy me when my ex-husband left stuff—clothing, papers, everything! —lying around on the floor. It really bugged me, so we put that in the agreement.

Announcer: Article 1c: Cleaning Up. Nothing will be left on the floor over night. Everything must be cleaned up and put away before going to bed.

Jane: Then I know it's clear to Bob what my expectations are.

Reporter: I'm sure that some people hearing this report will think that this contract isn't very romantic.

Announcer: Article 2: Sleeping. We will go to bed at 11:00 P.M. and wake up at 6:30 A.M., except on weekends.

Bob: Well, we disagree. We think it's very romantic. This contract shows that we sat down and talked, and really tried to understand the other person. A lot of problems occur in a marriage when people don't talk about what they want.

Jane: That's right! When we disagreed about something, we worked out a solution that was good for both of us. I would much rather have Bob really listen to me and understand my needs than give me a bunch of flowers or a box of candy.

Announcer: Article 4: Children. We will wait two years after our marriage to start having children. We will have no more than three children. After the first child, the spouse who makes less money will stop working to take care of the children.

Reporter: Other people may feel that some of these rules sound like a business agreement. A lot of them are concerned in some way with money . . . even the rules about having children talk about money.

Jane: In our experience, disagreements about money can cause a lot of problems in a marriage, so we talked about how we want to spend our money and put that in the agreement.

Announcer: Article 5: Money. Bob and Jane can each spend up to $100 per week on whatever they want. To spend more than $100 dollars per week, both Bob and Jane must agree about what they will buy.

Reporter: So, do you spend a lot of time checking to see if the other person is following the rules? Arguing?

Jane: No, not at all.

Bob: A lot couples argue because they don't understand each other's expectations. I think we spend less time arguing than most couples because we both know what the other person expects.

Announcer: Article 6: Communication. We will spend at least 15–30 minutes per day talking to each other without doing anything else.

Jane: Yes, we can spend our time doing things we enjoy and just being with each other.

Reporter: What happens if one of you breaks a rule?

Bob: Well, that's in our agreement, too.

Announcer: Article 13: Breaking Rules. If you break a rule, you must apologize and do something nice for the other person to make up for it.

Jane: Yeah, like one rule that Bob broke. . . .

Announcer: Article 7: Driving. If we are driving and get lost for more that five minutes, we will ask for directions.

Jane: We were driving to a friend's wedding, and we got lost. I wanted to stop at a gas station to ask for directions, but Bob said that he was sure he could figure it out. Well, to make a long story short, we drove forty miles in the wrong direction and ended up being late for the wedding.

Bob: So I took her out to dinner. I knew what I should do to apologize. That's a problem that many couples have . . . not knowing how to apologize.

Jane: Of course, I was still angry because he broke the rule.

Announcer: Article 9: Anger. If we get angry, we will go into separate rooms to cool off. We will not yell or use abusive language with each other.

Jane: But I felt better because he did something nice for me to make up for it.

Reporter: Do you plan to update your agreement at all? What if things change in your life and a rule doesn't work anymore?

Bob: That's also part of our agreement.

Announcer: Article 14: Changes to the agreement. Once a year, within thirty days of our anniversary, we will review this agreement and make any necessary changes.

Reporter: Do you think other couples should follow your example and write marriage agreements of their own?

Bob: It's a lot of work to write the agreement, but I think it could be useful to a lot of people.

Jane: Maybe there would be fewer divorces if everyone had to do this.

C. *Listening for Details*

(repeat Section 3B)

D. *Listening between the Lines*

EXCERPT 1

Bob: Yes, we found that many problems are caused when a person has different expectations than his or her spouse. We wanted to talk about everything openly and honestly before we started living together.

Jane: Also, we both know how important it is to respect each other's pet peeves. Like, it used to really annoy me when my ex-husband left stuff—clothing, papers, everything!—lying around on the floor. It really bugged me, so we put that in the contract.

EXCERPT 2

Reporter: I'm sure that some people hearing this report will think that this contract isn't very romantic.

Announcer: Article 2: Sleeping. We will go to bed at 11:00 P.M. and wake up at 6:30 A.M., except on weekends.

Bob: Well, we disagree. We think it's very romantic. This contract shows that we sat down and talked, and really tried to understand the other person. A lot of problems occur in a marriage when people don't talk about what they want.

Jane: That's right! When we disagreed about something, we worked out a solution that was good for both of us. I would much rather have Bob really listen to me and understand my needs than give me a bunch of flowers or a box of candy.

EXCERPT 3

Reporter: So, do you spend a lot of time checking to see if the other person is following the rules? Arguing?

Jane: No, not at all.

Bob: A lot couples argue because they don't understand each other's expectations. I think we spend less time arguing than most couples because we both know what the other person expects.

Announcer: Article 6: Communication. We will spend at least 15–30 minutes per day talking to each other without doing anything else.

Jane: Yes, we can spend our time doing things we enjoy and just being with each other.

4. LISTENING TWO: Reactions to the Marriage Agreement

Person 1: This contract? No way. I would never do this. It's not very romantic. I think that if you really love someone, you don't need to write all these things down. You just learn how to make your spouse happy and talk about problems when they come up.

Person 2: It might be a good idea, but I think this contract has too many details. For example, the rule about going to sleep at 11:00 P.M. What if one spouse wasn't sleepy or wanted to watch the news? That would be breaking a rule. It's silly. You can't plan every detail in your life.

Person 3: I think it's a great idea! I bet there would be a lot fewer divorces if everyone did this. Most couples don't know how to talk about their problems. They let small things annoy them until they finally blow up. Then they fight, but they don't know how to say "I'm sorry" afterwards. A contract like this would teach couples how to talk about their problems.

Person 4: I'm a lawyer, and I can tell you that this isn't a legal contract. What I mean is, if you went to court and said, "I want a divorce because my wife didn't use a shopping list to buy groceries," well, the judge would not give you a divorce for that reason. So legally, this contract has no power.

Person 5: I think the contract could be useful to help couples decide if they really should get married. A lot of couples get married because of their romantic feelings towards the other person, but they don't look carefully at who the person is. I think this contract would make both people think carefully about whether they should get married.

5. REVIEWING LANGUAGE

A. *Exploring Language: Contrastive Stress*

1. <u>Jane</u> will do the grocery shopping.
2. Jane will <u>always</u> use a shopping list.
3. Nothing will be left on the floor in the <u>bedroom</u>.
4. We will go to bed at <u>11:00</u> P.M.
5. We will wait <u>two</u> years to have children.
6. Bob <u>and</u> Jane can spend up to $100 dollars per week.
7. We will spend 30 minutes a day <u>talking</u> with each other.
8. If we are <u>driving</u> and get lost, we will ask for directions.
9. If we get angry, we will go into <u>separate</u> rooms to cool off.
10. Once a year, we will <u>update</u> this agreement.